Colorado HI-WAYS and BY-WAYS

A COMPREHENSIVE GUIDE TO PICTURESQUE TRAILS AND TOURS

by MARIAN TALMADGE and IRIS GILMORE

ISBN: 0-87108-079-6

© 1967, 1975 by Marian Talmadge and Iris Gilmore

Third Edition

1 2 3 4 5 6 7 8 9

Printed in the U.S.A.

PART 1

TABLE OF CONTENTS

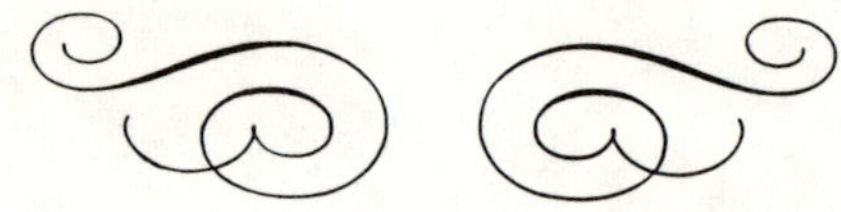

COLORADO

Gold was discovered in COLORADO (then Kansas Territory) in 1858, and by 1859 the "rush to the Rockies" was under way.

At first all the people who came were interested only in washing the precious yellow metal out of the streams and rivers, or grubbing it out of the mountain sides. But soon many persons found there was more in this high western country than hard yellow gold.

Business sprang up; fields were tilled and lush crops resulted. The clear exhilarating air brought health to many. Great cattle ranches were established. Railroads were built, and by 1876 another state—COLORADO—was added to the UNION.

The history of the state predates the discovery of gold, however. Geological evidence shows that millions of years ago this was tropical terrain. Indians and vast animal herds roamed here in historic times. The Spanish Conquistadores were the first white men to see it.

Then came the mountain men and trappers, the explorers, and finally the gold rush exploded, followed by the immigrants who actually made the state prosper. There is still gold to be found in COLORADO. Yes, hard, yellow stuff in the seams of undiscovered lodes in mountains, canyons and peaks.

But other gold is here for the prospector, too: healthful, invigorating air; wide acres for planting; beautiful towns and cities; grazing land for cattle. And last of all—but certainly not the least—is the beauty and awe-inspiring scenery and the year-round sports to attract both the visitor and the native. Where else can you find anything so precious as during the autumn when the mountain sides are covered with aspen gold?

Denver

By-Way Tour No. 1

Nature has been kind to DENVER—Mile High City—Queen City of the Plains—Gateway to the Rocky Mountain Empire.

Here people live, work and play in a climate which is dry, healthful and exhilarating. Over 300 days of bright sunshine a year combined with cool summer nights and a year-round moderate temperature makes DENVER the envy of many areas.

Wide green lawns, sprinkled by water from sparkling mountain streams, are a hallmark of this western metropolis. Broad tree-lined streets make the city an oasis where the high plains meet the mountains.

Within a day's pleasure driving radius are innumerable mountain trips affording the visitor every kind of pleasure—snow-capped mountain peaks, slopes heavily wooded with ponderosa pine, blue spruce and quaking aspen at their height of beauty in the autumn.

Fields of wild flowers carpet the hillsides, rushing mountain streams provide excellent fishing. There are trails for hikers and horseback riders, and lakes in which to swim, boat, water ski and fish.

Within an hour's drive from the city is some of the finest powder snow in the world for the ski enthusiast. Fan out in any direction from the city and the rockhound and collector of ancient artifacts will be rewarded. It is a shutterbug's paradise because of the blue, blue sky, white puffy clouds and innumerable picturesque scenes of high mountain peaks, flashing streams, colorful rocks and handsome terrain.

Our By-Way tour of the city starts at the gold-domed Capitol Building which commands CAPITOL HILL. Highlights include the imposing Grand Staircase which is a marvel of exquisite craftsmanship, the magnificent Rotunda with sixteen stunning stained glass portraits making up the COLORADO HALL OF FAME. In addition there are eight colorful murals which tell the history of water in COLORADO.

Your attention is called to the colorful red onyx used in the pilasters and wainscoting on the top three floors. It is rare COLORADO onyx never duplicated anywhere in the world, quarried near BEULAH, COLORADO, and the entire supply was used in this building.

From the Observation Tower within the dome is the best place to get a bird's-eye view of Metropolitan DENVER. To the west is the unsurpassed panorama of the theatrical mountain backdrop stretching from PIKES PEAK on the south to LONGS PEAK on the north—cobalt blue mountains with snowy tops etched into the skyline.

To the east flow the high plains from where the immigrants came, mostly in covered wagons. Surrounding DENVER are its lovely suburban towns.

Directly in front of the CAPITOL is CIVIC CENTER with its splendid landscape gardening, statuary and distinctive architecture. Due west is the graceful DENVER CITY AND COUNTY BUILDING housing municipal administrative offices.

Other interesting places around the center are the imposing new PUBLIC LIBRARY with its outstanding collection of Western Americana in the WESTERN HISTORY ROOM, the DENVER ART MUSEUM, HOSPITALITY HOUSE dispensing information for visitors, and the UNITED STATES MINT where tours are conducted.

Our By-Way tour now swings to the business section which has drawn much recent interest. Long a city with a low skyline, this is now being changed with the addition of such skyscrapers as the MILE HIGH CENTER (Denver-United States National Bank), the DENVER CLUB with the EISENHOWER CHAPEL, the SECURITY LIFE BUILDING, the FIRST NATIONAL BANK, the PETROLEUM BUILDING, and the FARMERS' UNION BUILDING. The unique MAY D&F STORE has an outside ice skating rink. The BROWN PALACE HOTEL is

The State Capitol in Denver ▶

DENVER CLUB, SECURITY LIFE (outside glass-enclosed elevator), UNITED BANK OF DENVER, FIRST NATIONAL BANK, LINCOLN CENTER, WESTERN FEDERAL SAVINGS, COLORADO NATIONAL BANK and COLORADO STATE BANK to name some. The attractive BROWN PALACE HOTEL is still an uptown landmark dating from the early days.

Urban renewal has removed many of the buildings in downtown DENVER. However, the old DANIELS AND FISHER TOWER, copied from the Campanile in Venice, Italy, is still a landmark. New buildings include BROOKS TOWERS, CURRIGAN CONVENTION CENTER, PARK CENTRAL, PRUDENTIAL PLAZA and the FEDERAL RESERVE BANK. SAKURA TOWERS for low income families dominates a square block of Japanese stores, restaurants and the BUDDHIST CHURCH. LARIMER SQUARE between 14th and 15th Streets on LARIMER STREET is a delightful restoration of old buildings housing picturesque restaurants, shops and theaters.

DENVER has over 100 named parks in the city in addition to about 25 mountain parks. CITY PARK in east DENVER contains the ZOO, the DENVER MUSEUM OF NATURAL HISTORY, and PHIPPS AUDITORIUM for entertainments and lectures.

WASHINGTON PARK is known for its exquisite flower gardens, the small house of EUGENE FIELD (famous poet), and the statue illustrating his poem, WYNKEN, BLYNKEN AND NOD. CHEESMAN PARK has a lovely Greek pavilion with a mountain finder showing the names and locations of all the principal peaks in the mountains to the west. Nearby is DENVER BOTANIC GARDENS, a real show place.

From the cultural and entertainment standpoint, DENVER offers the DENVER SYMPHONY ORCHESTRA; ELITCH'S GARDENS, with its famous summer theatre; BONFILS MEMORIAL THEATRE (Little Theatre); LAKESIDE AMUSEMENT PARK; the COLISEUM (the National Western Stock Show operates here in January); MILE-HI STADIUM; CENTENNIAL TURF CLUB and MILE HIGH KENNEL CLUB.

In addition to fine public and private secondary schools, higher education includes the UNIVERSITY OF COLORADO MEDICAL SCHOOL and EXTENSION CENTER, the UNIVERSITY OF DENVER, REGIS COLLEGE, COLORADO WOMAN'S COLLEGE, and LORETTO HEIGHTS COLLEGE.

Churches of all faiths are found in the city with two cathedrals and large downtown churches and many new churches built in stunning new architectural forms.

DENVER is often called the "second capital" of the UNITED STATES because there are more Federal offices here than in any other American city except Washington, D.C. Downtown are the POST OFFICE and the FEDERAL BUILDINGS. FEDERAL CENTER near the foothills to the west houses the BUREAU OF RECLAMATION and many other federal agencies. FITZSIMONS ARMY HOSPITAL is located just east of AURORA, and LOWRY AIR FORCE BASE is to the southeast of the city.

There are many beautiful residential areas within DENVER itself — the remaining old mansions on CAPITOL HILL, Seventh Avenue Parkway, Park Hill, Hilltop, Crestmoor, the Polo Grounds, and Belcaro have some of the real showplaces of the city.

DENVER has an interesting history. The first gold strike in the Rockies occurred in 1859 where LITTLE DRY CREEK enters the SOUTH PLATTE RIVER starting the first "rush to the Rockies" in 1859, also called "Pikes Peak or Bust."

Now the city is one of the fastest growing in the country. With the increase in size, its efficiency and popularity are sought as host to thousands of visitors.

The Denver Museum of Natural History

The Prospector's Trail

By-Way Tour No. 2

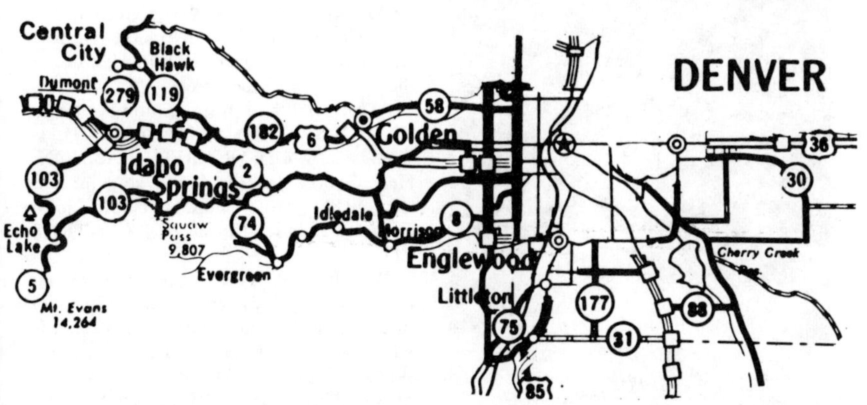

"The Prospectors' Trail" is considered one of the most popular and rewarding trips in Colorado. This area includes as varied, spectacular and easily accessible scenic spots as anywhere in the state. Highways that are marvels in engineering take you along canyons into the foothills to famous gold mining country, into the heart of a national forest with its thousands of pine-clad acres, skirts precipitous cliffs, winds down granite-walled corridors of turbulent mountain streams and climbs up to the highest auto road in the world.

Our By-Way tour leaves DENVER on U. S. 6 or 40. At their junction they join Interstate 70, which you will follow for about two miles.

At the next junction leave I 70 and continue south along the "Hogback" road (State 93) a few miles to unique RED ROCKS PARK. Scrubby green juniper trees, young when Columbus discovered America, contrast sharply with the weird and spectacularly tilted red sandstone rocks which make up this striking geological spectacle.

Owned by the city of DENVER as one of its many Mountain Parks, RED ROCKS, in addition to its stirring beauty, offers a world-renowned outdoor natural amphitheater seating 10,000 persons. It has scientifically perfect acoustics and provides an inimitable setting for summer concerts. Here symphony, ballet, operatic and dramatic programs as well as Easter Sunrise services are performed for ecstatic audiences.

Two miles south is MORRISON, homesteaded in 1870 and considered the gateway to DENVER'S MOUNTAIN PARK SYSTEM. The old pink sandstone schoolhouse and Hill Crest Inn with its quaint two-story piazza are landmarks.

State 74 from MORRISON climbs around the shoulder of the foothills and follows BEAR CREEK CANYON.

KITTREDGE is home base for many people working in DENVER who commute each day.

EVERGREEN looks like a postcard village dropped between velvety green mountains. It is the center of choice mountain resorts and dude ranches, shops, and elegant summer homes. EVERGREEN LAKE has excellent fishing, and there is a public golf grounds nearby.

Our By-Way tour continues on State 74 from EVERGREEN through DEDISSE PARK, homesteaded by a French trapper in 1859. Next is BERGEN PARK founded in 1860 and a favorite picnic spot. Rocks from the old Bergen home-

Picturesque Echo Lake at the foot of Mt. Evans

stead cabin are in the marker near the road junction. Originally this was a toll road to CENTRAL CITY and GEORGE-TOWN built by the territorial government, but travelers going to religious services or funerals paid no fee. Nearby is FILLIUS PARK, another picnic area.

State 74 takes our By-Way tour up a spectacularly beautiful road over SQUAW PASS (Squaw Pass Fire Lookout Station may be reached by foot trail), and JUNI-PER PASS through ARAPAHOE NATIONAL FOREST. This is a favorite road during the fall to see aspen in their golden splendor.

ECHO LAKE, at the foot of MT. EVANS, has many picnic and cooking facilities facing the lake.

A side trip 8.7 miles starts left up the highest auto road in the world. A succession of hairpin curves, the well-constructed highway leads to snow-fed SUM-MIT LAKE nestled in a Jovian cup which is actually the cone of an old volcano, and no one knows how deep the lake is.

The summit of MT. EVANS is 14,260 feet above sea level and you can gaze at panoramic wonders of grandeur from a stunning glassed-in observation room. Photogenic vistas lure you. PIKES PEAK seems just a stone's throw to the southeast. SOUTH PARK is a green handkerchief edged with snow-capped peaks. LONGS PEAK rises majestically to the north. To the west are the glacial altitudes of the CONTINENTAL DIVIDE piercing the blue skyline. DENVER and the high plains to the east appear in microscopic wonder.

Back to ECHO LAKE our By-Way tour descends through imposing granite-walled CHICAGO CREEK CANYON to ID-AHO SPRINGS. The bright green leaves of the kinnikinnick with orange-red berries in the fall cover the hillsides under the spruce and aspen trees.

A pictorial and historic mining town, IDAHO SPRINGS (U.S. 6 & 40) is strung along CLEAR CREEK CANYON. Here George Jackson found gold in January, 1859, five months before John Gregory found it in nearby CENTRAL CITY.

IDAHO SPRINGS' world-famous radium hot springs and swimming pool make it a favorite haven. During the winter it is a popular week-end resort for skiers at nearby ARAPAHOE BASIN, LOVELAND and BERTHOUD SKI BASINS.

Another By-Way tour follows I 70 west from IDAHO SPRINGS two miles to where FALL RIVER empties into CLEAR CREEK. Leave the highway and follow a winding, graded road for ten miles to a ghost town, ALICE. From here you can hike up an old wagon road to ST. MARY'S GLACIER and see ice that was formed thousands of years ago during the ice age slowly working its way down to form ST. MARY'S LAKE.

Back at IDAHO SPRINGS our By-Way tour picks up State 279 and follows a thrilling old-time mountain road which loops, twists and swings its way up VIR-GINIA CANYON. Today it's a new, safe road replacing the steep, dangerous early stage route whose scars can still be seen.

After "looping the loops" up to 9500 feet altitude, RUSSELL GULCH is reached. Green Russell with his party of several hundred southerners discovered gold here in 1859 and they panned more than $20,000 in this vicinity. By September 900 men were panning gold that averaged $35,000 a week.

The road takes you higher past innumerable ore dumps and mine shafts gophered into the mountain sides, up to a high ridge known as QUARTZ HILL. As you top this hill you see fabulous CENTRAL CITY below you folded into

Central City as we see it today ▶

TELLER HOUSE
OWL
XXXX COFFEE

a three-cornered canyon.

The houses perch precariously above each other on reinforced terraces of cobblestones. Often called the "Little Kingdom of Gilpin" and "the richest square mile on earth" because $85 million in gold was mined here in the '60's, CENTRAL CITY at that time was the second largest city in Colorado.

Culture arrived in the form of the OPERA HOUSE where such famous theatrical persons as Edwin Booth, Janaus Chek, Lotta Crabtree, Modjeska and Christine Nilsson trod the boards.

President Ulysses S. Grant stayed at the TELLER HOUSE in 1873 and walked from his stagecoach into the hotel across a sidewalk paved with silver bricks worth $13,000.

CENTRAL CITY has known two booms—once in 1859 when it became a scene of feverish mining activity and the scars still show where man ripped up the earth in a frantic search for gold.

The second boom started in 1932 when the semi-ghost town was aroused from its Rip Van Winkle sleep to a new life with strong emphasis on culture.

The CENTRAL CITY FESTIVAL which attracts thousands of visitors each summer produces operas and plays in the renovated stone OPERA HOUSE. During July and August you may rub shoulders with world-famous actors and singers who consider it a privilege to perform in the "LITTLE KINGDOM OF GILPIN," as CENTRAL CITY is called.

The famous Opera House in Central City

At the top of wooden stairs above EUREKA STREET (now RICKETSON BLVD.) is the MASONIC TEMPLE, well worth a visit to see the unique art painted by an itinerant artist in 1864.

Back along State 287, past a wilderness of tailings hundreds of feet high, our By-Way tour takes us along a rutted wagon trail to GLORY HOLE. Here ore was mined in a gigantic pit 1000 feet across and 300 feet deep in many places.

Another mile or so is NEVADAVILLE, a true ghost town, which once rivaled CENTRAL CITY in population. Today only a cluster of decaying false fronts and tumbled-down shacks are reminders of yesterday's glory.

Anywhere in this area the old mining dumps are "happy hunting grounds" for the rockhounds.

From CENTRAL CITY our By-Way tour follows State 279 east past a marker showing where John Gregory discovered gold in May, 1859. BLACKHAWK is the name of the village which hugs the steep canyon walls. More Victorian houses are here, trimmed with the ubiquitous "gingerbread."

At the junction of State 119 our By-Way turns right, following the creek.

At the junction of U. S. 6 go straight ahead. Here engineers lacked space to hang a road so tunnels were blasted through the mountains. Most of this highway is built over the old railroad bed of the Colorado & Southern Railroad.

At the junction of U. S. 6 and I 70 our By-Way tour turns left and follows I 70 over FLOYD HILL, once a steep stage road.

You will pass GENESEE MOUNTAIN PARK (owned by DENVER) which is a favorite picnic spot. A couple of miles east is a junction. Our By-Way leads to the left to LOOKOUT MOUNTAIN where William F. Cody "Buffalo Bill," his wife and step-son, Johnny Baker, are buried. PAHASKA TEPEE, nearby museum, houses many of his mementos.

Our tour then picks up the "LARIAT TRAIL" down LOOKOUT MOUNTAIN, a series of spectacular switchbacks or hairpin curves which follow one of the first wagon roads into the mountains. It offers an awe-inspiring view of GOLDEN, TABLE MOUNTAIN, DENVER, and the high plains to the east.

From GOLDEN, our By-Way tour follows U. S. 6 to DENVER.

The Black Forest

By-Way Tour No. 3

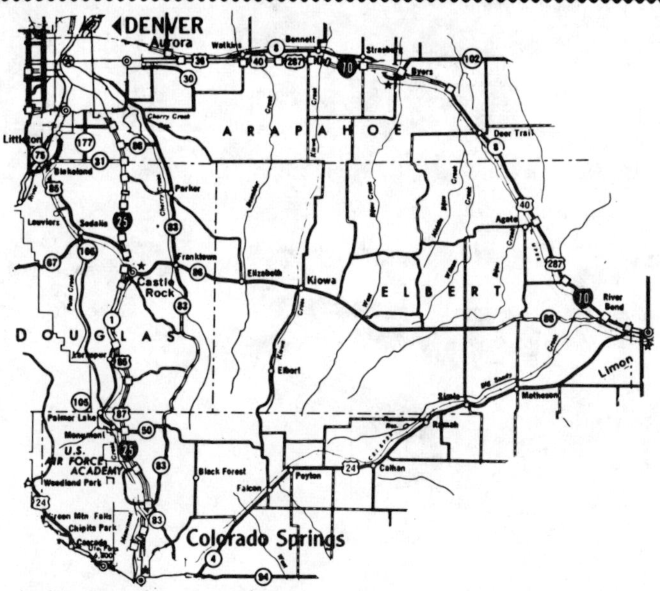

One of the least known and least traveled areas in Colorado is that back country section known as the BLACK FOREST where great stands of virgin Ponderosa pine darken the hillsides and give the area its name. Your time budget will determine your length of stay. Anyone of several routes will make a pleasant day's drive using DENVER or COLORADO SPRINGS as a starting point.

A prelude to the mountains, which form a dramatic backdrop to the west, the BLACK FOREST includes clear creeks and miniature canyons, rocky knolls and numerous arroyos—all adding their charm. Although over-shadowed by the towering Rockies, the BLACK FOREST has much to offer the visitor who likes to get "off the beaten path."

While the buffalo no longer roam these wooded hillsides and the high plains to the east, there are still herds of antelope, some deer, as well as long-eared jack rabbits, and prairie dogs living in their miniature "towns."

Bands of Ute, Arapahoe, and Kiowa Indians fought over these favorite hunting grounds before the white man came.

The old "Trappers Trail" from SANTA FE, NEW MEXICO to FORT LARAMIE, WYOMING bisected the BLACK FOREST through present day FRANKTOWN and PARKER following CHERRY CREEK to its juncture with the SOUTH PLATTE in DENVER.

The gold rush of 1859 (PIKES PEAK OR BUST!) brought eager gold seekers along the SMOKY HILL TRAIL (U. S. 40, State 86 and 83). This trail which the BUTTERFIELD and WELLS FARGO EXPRESS later followed, bordered BIG SANDY CREEK from the KANSAS line to RIVER BEND, then swung west through KUHN'S CROSSING, KIOWA, ELIZABETH, HILLTOP and PARKER, down CHERRY CREEK to DENVER. A State Historical marker records PARKER as old TWENTY-MILE STATION on the trail.

Known as the "Starvation Trail," it was a shorter route to the gold fields than either the OVERLAND TRAIL to the north or the SANTA FE TRAIL to the south. But lack of water and game made it much more hazardous.

Cattle grazing in the Black Forest

Dreams of the empire builders are buried in the abandoned cinder railroad bed which can still be followed southeast from DENVER through SULLIVAN, PARKER, HILLTOP, ELIZABETH, ELBERT, EASTONVILLE to FALCON (State 83 and 157).

The COLORADO AND SOUTHERN RAILROAD hoped to build to the Texas Gulf Coast and NEW ORLEANS last century, but got only as far as PUEBLO in 1881, and the road was abandoned in 1936.

In addition to the paved highways which encircle it, the BLACK FOREST is criss-crossed with State Highways 83, 79, 157 and 86 and many well-graded county roads service prosperous ranches. The rolling countryside is studded with white-faced Herefords and stubby-legged Black Angus cattle fattening on the curly native buffalo and grama grasses. Huge barns testify to the lush wild hay which covers the creek bottoms.

One of the most spectacular wild flower shows in the country occurs in late May and June, a month before the same kind of flowers appear in the neighboring mountains. Pink penstemons, purple larkspur, blue lupine, yellow pea flowers, white sand lilies, and the creamy bells of the spiky green yucca or Spanish bayonet cover acres of rolling hillsides and the pine-needle-covered forest floor. The early pioneers called the yucca "soapweed" because they learned from the Indians how to make soap from its roots.

Today's visitors will find good picnic spots, hiking, and horseback riding. For rockhounds there are plenty of petrified wood specimens available in the dry creek bottoms and arroyos or gullies eroded by the flash floods which occur after summer downpours or cloudbursts.

The collector of Indian arrowheads and artifacts can find specimens near the old water holes, buffalo wallows, and "dust blowouts" where the dust storms of the 1930's scooped out depressions where the Indians camped many years ago.

These "happy hunting grounds" are found both in the BLACK FOREST and in the high plains crossed by U.S. Highways 40, 287 and 24. BURLINGTON near the KANSAS line, which was built on the site of an ancient Indian camp ground and prehistoric animal rendezvous, has added to many collections.

A few miles west of the BLACK FOREST is MONUMENT (Interstate 25) where old FORT McSHANE was built to protect the great freighters moving up the trail from SANTA FE. Nearby are many picturesque geological formations eroded by wind and rain: TEAPOT ROCK, ELEPHANT ROCK, PINNACLE and MUSHROOM PARKS. The FORESTRY SERVICE maintains a nursery here where seedlings are raised to replant the burned areas in the mountains which forest fires have destroyed.

PALMER LAKE (State 105), named for WILLIAM JACKSON PALMER who built the DENVER & RIO GRANDE RAILROAD, is one of the oldest summer resorts in COLORADO. The town is now booming because of the UNITED STATES AIR FORCE ACADEMY built nearby. The famous PALMER LAKE YULE LOG HUNT draws hundreds of visitors each December on the Sunday before Christmas.

From PALMER LAKE State 105 goes through PERRY PARK, a bit of old NEW ENGLAND, to SEDALIA. Legend says Black Bart, a stage holdup man of the '70's, buried his last haul on the J Ranch near SEDALIA. A bandit with a sense of humor, he usually left a bit of doggerel verse in the WELLS FARGO EXPRESS boxes which he robbed signed "Po-8" which translated meant "Po-ate" or "poet."

Another pleasant and leisurely route is through LARKSPUR (MONKEY ROCK to the west) and GREENLAND. Vivid jagged rocks and colorful scrub oak, willow and pinon pine brighten the country-side.

CASTLE ROCK (Interstate 25) was named for the huge butte nearby which resembles a chessboard castle, a well-known Indian and trapper landmark. It was first mentioned in MAJOR STEPHEN LONG'S JOURNAL in 1820 and painted by the expedition's artist.

State 177 takes off from U.S. 87 between CASTLE ROCK and SEDALIA through DANIELS PARK. Here WILDCAT POINT affords a spectacular panoramic view of DENVER and the SOUTH PLATTE VALLEY to the north and west. DEVILS HEAD, PIKES PEAK, the SPANISH PEAKS and the CULEBRA range are to the south.

HAPPY CANYON, as this area is called, was given to the Utes as a reservation soon after DENVER was settled. A granite marker notes that KIT CARSON, famous frontiersman, was fatally stricken here when he camped enroute home after his final trip to Washington to intercede for his Indian friends. He was carried to FORT LYON where he died.

"Council of War" rocks near Monument

Ghost Town Trails

By-Way Tour No. 4

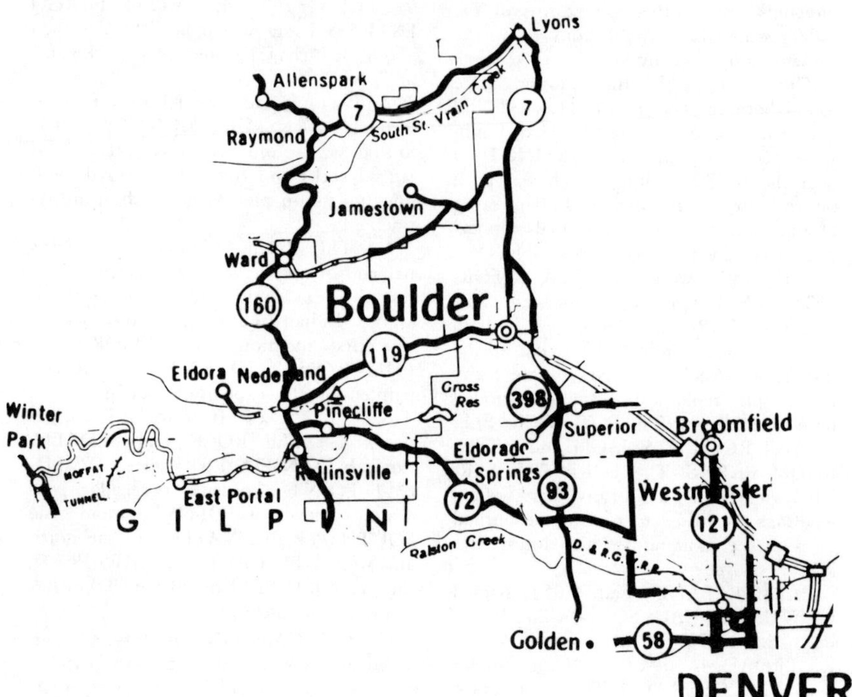

Some of the earliest and richest mining camps in the state were established in the hills back of BOULDER. Today most of them are either ghost towns or summer resorts with an occasional mine still being worked sporadically.

This By-Way tour is planned to see many of these camps with the idea of giving the visitor an opportunity to take away with him what he will. Perhaps he'll snap colored photographs to remind him of a pleasant summer holiday. Or he'll add to his mineral collection or pick up some Indian artifacts. Maybe he'll take away only a memory of quiet mountain by-ways which once boomed as the miners scratched frantically for elusive gold.

Our By-Way tour leaves DENVER on U.S. 6 or 40 continuing on U.S. 6 to GOLDEN. first capital of COLORADO TERRITORY.

Be sure to see the COLORADO SCHOOL OF MINES, one of the foremost mining schools in the world attracting students from many foreign countries. They have an outstanding collection of minerals in the MINING BUILDING. The JEFFERSON COUNTY MUSEUM is located in the City Hall.

You take State 58 north past RALSTON RESERVOIR turning left on State 72 and following COAL CREEK CANYON past WONDERVU and PINECLIFF to the junction with State 119 at ROLLINSVILLE.

A most desirable side trip from ROLLINSVILLE follows SOUTH BOULDER CREEK and the railroad past TOLLAND, a ghost town, as far as EAST PORTAL and the entrance to the MOFFAT TUNNEL. Here the streamliners enter the famed tunnel, a six-mile bore through JAMES PEAK, a marvel in railroad engineering.

Ahead of you is the "Giant's Ladder," a series of cutbacks resembling the rungs of a ladder. It's the old roadbed where the railroad used to run before the tunnel was built. At ANTELOPE SIDING, the powerful Mallet steam engines waited to help "push" the trains over CORONA PASS. Old time railroaders will tell you that the engines began to "bark" when they started this climb. After the railroad abandoned this route, it was called the road to nowhere. Now that label is obsolete.

As you top a ridge, YANKEE DOODLE LAKE stretches before you tucked against rocky cliffs and surrounded by pine trees. There are twenty accessible lakes here with excellent trout fishing.

The road horseshoes around the lake and climbs past DIXIE LAKE. You can see the old Rollins Trail jackknifing east up the hill and cutting straight west over the pass.

The terrain changes as you climb. The pines and spruce are left behind. Bright mountain flowers nod in the cool breeze. Tundra replaces grass, and finally there is only bare rock as you realize you are nearing the "top of the world."

As you swing around a curve, there is NEEDLE'S EYE TUNNEL and beyond is a trestle, then another. Now you are at the top of CORONA PASS on the CONTINENTAL DIVIDE. Long vistas spread in every direction as you become aware that this is a never-to-be-forgotten experience. It's a photographer's delight.

You may return on the same road. An alternate route is to drop down quickly through spruce and aspen forests to WINTER PARK (U. S. 40) and return to DENVER via BERTHOUD PASS.

Our By-Way tour returns to ROLLINSVILLE, then follows State 119 to NEDERLAND, named by a Dutch syndicate.

A side trip three miles west leads you

The Moffat Road near the crest of the mountain range

to ELDORA, a semi-ghost town, now a summer resort and ski area. Another side road from NEDERLAND leads to CARIBOU, famous for its valuable silver lodes. Now only crumbling stone walls and windswept buildings show where the town once stood.

In the summer months the fields are bright with pink pentstemon, creamy mariposa lilies, purple lupine and gold pea-flowers. Magenta fireweed covers the burns where forest fires have taken their toll.

Our By-Way sweeps northward through densely forested country.

This is glacier country where trails lead to various ones. The most popular trip is past the old FOURTH OF JULY MINE to ARAPAHOE GLACIER, owned by the city of BOULDER for their water supply.

The houses at WARD, on State 160, hang precariously on the steep slopes of the canyons. The fireplace of the WARD HOTEL is built of gold ore.

Here State 7 will take you north to ESTES PARK only 22 miles away. Our By-Way tour turns east on State 7 to LYONS, then south on the same highway to BOULDER.

BOULDER is the starting point for many By-Way tours to abandoned mining camps and ghost towns along old trails which criss-cross the hills behind the city.

LEFT-HAND CANYON was named for Niwot (meaning Left-hand), an Indian chief. The road leaves State 7 about eleven miles north of BOULDER left through ALTONA. When the road forks, take the right hand fork to SPRINGDALE and JAMESTOWN (called JIMTOWN in the old days), then on to GRESHAM connecting finally with State 160.

The left hand fork on this same road takes you to GLENDALE, ROWENA, CAMP TOLCOTT into WARD on State 160.

A scenic circle trip out of BOULDER leads up BOULDER CANYON (State 119) to FOUR MILE CREEK ROAD. Turn right here following the creek to CRISMAN, then on to SALINA, making a sharp left turn following the creek to WALL STREET. (The other road is the shortest route to GOLD HILL.)

Go through WALL STREET with its delightful summer homes, to COPPER ROCK with its abandoned ore crushers to SUNSET, marked by an abandoned railroad boxcar.

Turn right on a curving trail road which joins the abandoned railroad grade, circles the shoulder of a hill and climbs to MT. ALTA which was once the goal of excursionists who rode the narrow gauge from BOULDER or DENVER for week-end outings. The old stone fireplace shows where the pavilion once stood. A couple of miles beyond is the county road where you turn left to go to WARD or right to GOLD HILL.

Our By-Way tour goes to GOLD HILL. Here is the BLUE BIRD LODGE where Eugene Field wrote "Casey's Table D'Hote" in 1882 when he worked for the DENVER TRIBUNE. A road straight north out of the delightful resort village will take you over LICK SKILLET HILL to the LEFT HAND CANYON ROAD.

Our route follows the county road east to SUNSHINE. Enroute you will catch glimpses of the plains, LONGMONT, the toll road, and even DENVER. Our By-Way follows SUNSHINE CANYON back to BOULDER.

One of the best known trips is up spectacular BOULDER CANYON to NEDERLAND. Originally this was a toll road built to service WARD, CARIBOU and other rich mining camps.

TUNGSTEN is another ghost town but of later vintage, founded during WORLD WAR I when tungsten was needed to harden steel. Next is beautiful BARKER RESERVOIR to your left, and directly above is NEDERLAND.

BOULDER, once a sleepy college town, has boomed with the advent of many businesses which have moved into the area including the Federal Bureau of Standards. It was founded in 1858 by gold seekers who camped at the mouth of BOULDER CANYON.

The residential sections—both old and new—are charming, built up against the picturesque mountains with a wide sweeping view of the high plains. The UNIVERSITY OF COLORADO has a strikingly beautiful campus with buildings of red sandstone quarried near LYONS.

A drive to the top of FLAGSTAFF MOUNTAIN is recommended to give you a breathtaking panoramic view of the entire area.

Our By-Way tour returns to DENVER via the DENVER-BOULDER TURNPIKE.

The High Plains

By-Way Tour No. 5

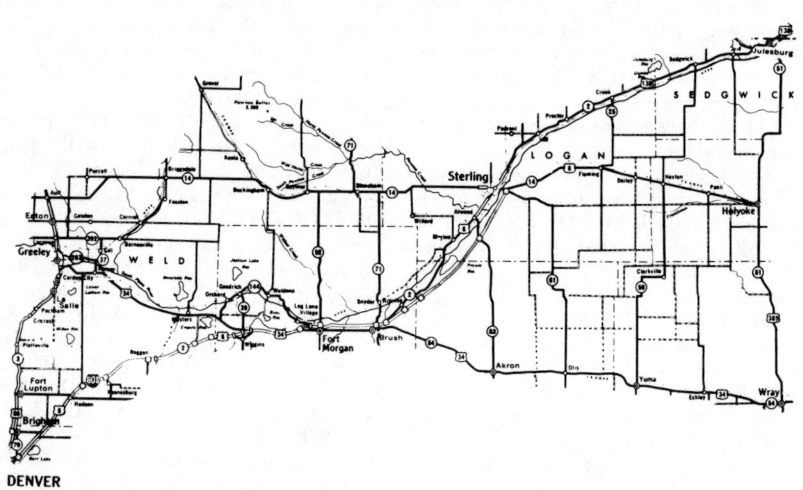

Pony Express—Overland Trail—Upper California Crossing—Leavenworth, Pikes Peak & Overland Express—Beecher Island Battlefield—Pawnee Buttes—Buffalo Bill—Union Colony. These are some of the names which conjure up the exciting days of the '49er's to California and the '59er's to Colorado, and the Indian Wars of the late 19th Century.

Our By-Way tour steps back into country steeped in stirring history. Four flags have flown over it as the country was passed back and forth among as many nations. Once a battleground, it is now a prosperous ranching and farming area.

The plains Indians—Arapahoes, Cheyennes and Sioux—claimed this area as their traditional hunting grounds and moved their lodgepoles from place to place following the herds of wild animals and were continuously struggling for possession of it among themselves.

The Spanish explorer, Pedro de Villesur, passed here in 1720. A century later Vasquez, Bent, Beckwourth and other mountain men and fur trappers built trading posts and followed the well-beaten trails.

The pathfinders, Fremont and Long, made use of this South Platte valley. Later, tales of fabulous gold strikes lured thousands of eager persons westward. Also, the cattle barons and the cowboys had their day on these great plains.

Finally the giant tide of settlers came to turn much of this vast prairie country into a garden spot.

Our By-Way tour starts from Denver, but the majority of eastern visitors enter from the east via U. S. Highways 6 or 34. From Denver follow I 80S northeast.

ROGGEN was the headquarters of "Painter's Pastures," one of the huge cattle companies founded in the early days by English money. WIGGINS was originally a fur-trading post started in 1838 by "Old Man Wiggins," a friend of Kit Carson.

FORT MORGAN was first a fur-trading post built by "Squawman" Sam Ashcroft, then it became a stage station for the OVERLAND EXPRESS.

The site of OLD FORT MORGAN is marked by a monument on Riverview Avenue. Now a prosperous agricultural and cattle center, FORT MORGAN is a lovely small town shaded by beautiful native and imported trees. A replica of old Fort Morgan is in the V.F.W. Museum.

A few miles beyond is BRUSH (I 80S & U.S. 34), another agricultural and cattle center with one of the largest feed yards in the nation. It was named for Jared Brush who established a cattle empire here in the early days.

Our By-Way tour goes east from BRUSH via U.S. 34 through AKRON and YUMA, also farm and cattle communities, across "dryland flats," home of giant jack rabbits, coyotes and antelope.

WRAY was built on moist river ground and keeps its green grass even in the driest summer weather. South from WRAY (about sixteen miles on a country road) is historic BEECHER ISLAND SITE on the Arickaree River. Here Colonel George Forsythe with 51 soldiers and scouts holed in for eight days against more than 1000 Indians led by Roman Nose, famous Cheyenne chief, who was killed in the battle.

Arrowheads as well as prehistoric animal bones and ancient Indian artifacts are still found in this vicinity. The dust storms of the '30's helped uncover many old water hole sites.

North of WRAY on State 51 is HOLYOKE.

Our By-Way tour follows State 51 north to JULESBURG, perhaps the most famous (or infamous) town on the OVERLAND TRAIL. A much-traveled town, it actually existed on four different sites. The present town lying among the broken hills in a curve of the South Platte river was settled in 1881 when the Union Pacific Railroad built a cutoff to DENVER. It is still a division point on the railroad as well as a trading center for a large agricultural region.

Before crossing the bridge over the South Platte to enter the town, turn left on a country road which follows approximately the OREGON - OVERLAND TRAIL.

The site of the second JULESBURG is about six miles west of State 51 and was the gathering place of cattle rustlers.

About nine miles west of State 51 is a marker showing the original site of OLD JULESBURG, named for Jules Beni, a Frenchman, who established a trading post here near the ford on the South Platte which became known as the "Upper California Crossing." This JULESBURG became famous as a PONY EXPRESS and OVERLAND EXPRESS STATION under the direction of "Jack" Slade who killed Jules after a personal feud. This first JULESBURG was burned to the ground by Indians in February, 1865.

Our By-Way tour now crosses the South Platte river to OVID (I 80S) and continues on State 27 to a railroad siding nearby called WEIR.

This was the site of the THIRD JULESBURG, once called the "wickedest little city east of the Rockies." It was a nest of saloons, gambling dens, dance halls, and its crowded streets were filled with soldiers, frontiersmen, gamblers, painted "ladies" and railroad huskies.

This is still good country in which to find Indian arrowheads and other artifacts. A country road leads east here into present-day JULESBURG. The Pioneer Museum in the basement of the Public Library (3 blocks north of U.S. 138 on Cedar street) has many relics from the three JULESBURGS and FORT SEDGWICK.

From JULESBURG our By-Way tour follows I 80S southwest through OVID, SEDGWICK and CROOK to ILIFF and STERLING, a modern city shaded by giant cottonwoods curved over the streets. This thrifty crossroads community is a railroad and trading center.

An interesting By-Way trip is State 14 straight west out of STERLING. An area of brown hills covered with sagebrush and a few rock outcroppings, attempts to farm this land did not meet with much success. The sun-drenched towns of STONEHAM and NEW RAYMER, with their weathered false-front buildings, look like something out of a TV Western or a Grade B movie.

A side trip on State 155, a graveled road through KEOTA, takes you 20 miles beyond to moody PAWNEE BUTTES, resembling a ship sailing on a dry sea. Early landmarks and Indian rendezvous, the BUTTES are good hunting grounds for the rockhound, not only for more recent Indian artifacts, but because of the prehistoric bones of such animals as horses and camels found here as early as 1875 by scientists from Yale University.

Back to BRIGGSDALE on State 14, another weather-beaten small western town. To the north is SEVEN CROSS HILL which was a lookout in the early days for the cowboys of the ranch where they watched for stray cattle, visitors and marauding Indians.

The road joins U. S. 85 at AULT, then south through EATON and LUCERNE to GREELEY, all farming communities.

Your alternate By-Way route from STERLING may follow U. S. 6 to AT-WOOD. Sixteen miles south on State 63 is the site of SUMMIT SPRINGS BAT-TLEGROUND where the last important Indian battle was fought in northeastern Colorado. The Cheyennes, led by Tall Bull, were defeated here by the U. S. Cavalry and their Pawnee scouts on July 11, 1869.

Next is MERINO. Follow U. S. 6 to BRUSH and continue on through FT. MORGAN. Here you will pick up I 80S for about four miles. Leave I 80S and take U. S. 34. About two miles beyond take State 39 north to ORCHARD, site of the first oil well drilled in eastern Colorado in 1918. This is excellent game country. During open season there are wild ducks and Canadian geese who in-habit the many reservoirs around here. Pheasant and antelope hunting is also popular, as well as fishing for bullheads, catfish, crappie, bass and perch.

South of MASTERS on a country road may be seen oyster shells at 4500 feet above sea level. Millions of years ago this country was the bottom of a great sea. Today the shells are ground up for chicken feed.

U. S. 34 now swings close to the South Platte river again, center of fertile irri-gated fields to KERSEY.

To the south of the road is the site of OLD FORT LATHAM, another sta-tion on the trail, and an important ford-ing place on the river. Some immigrants came this way, then swung north on the LARAMIE TRAIL rather than ford the South Platte at the treacherous Upper California Crossing near JULESBURG.

To the north of the highway at the junction of the South Platte and the Cache la Poudre rivers is SCOUT ISLAND, a favorite picnic spot.

U. S. 34 joins U. S. 85 at GREELEY. From here our By-Way tour swings south and west via LASALLE, PLATTEVILLE, FORT VASQUEZ, FORT LUPTON and BRIGHTON to DENVER.

Overland Trail Museum east of Sterling

Mining Camp Trails

By-Way Tour No. 6

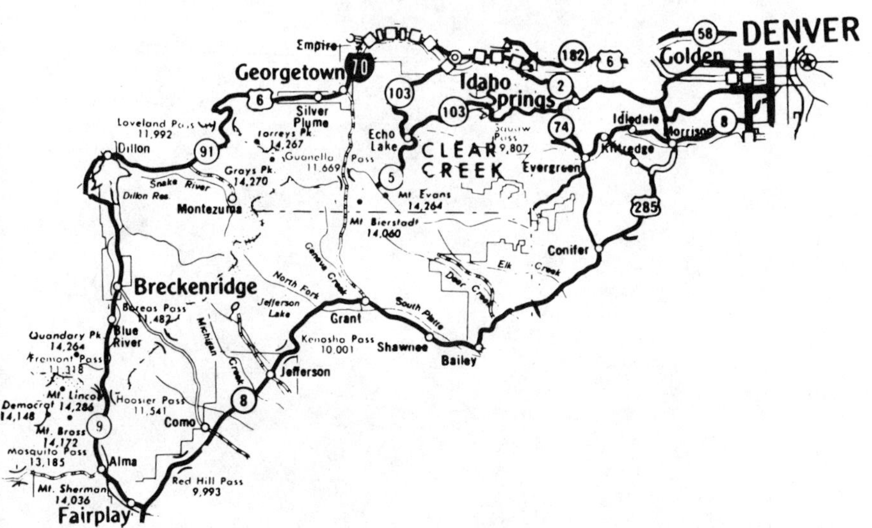

This By-Way tour takes you through historic country which in its hey-day catered to thousands of miners bent on making their fortunes in the gold and silver mines which honeycomb the area.

Every road you follow was once a stagecoach trail or railroad grade. The country was well-known to the Indians, particularly the Utes who claimed it as their rightful home.

Here is a paradise for the vacationist who wants to fish, ride horseback, hike, camp, explore ghost towns, look for rock specimen, take pictures, or just rest. Any and all of these activities may be found in abundance.

Our By-Way tour leaves DENVER on U. S. 285 to MORRISON. Curving up and out of the village, the highway slashes the high ridge between TURKEY and BEAR CREEKS.

Our By-Way swings rather abruptly into narrow TURKEY CREEK CANYON high above the turbulent creek, with its heavy stand of lodgepole pines on the slopes to the south.

For a scenic side trip take the first road to the right winding through PARMALEE GULCH and INDIAN HILLS past PENCE PARK (DENVER MOUNTAIN PARK) to KITTREDGE.

Our By-Way tour continues on U. S. 285. State 73 to the right is a scenic back road to EVERGREEN.

Next is SHAFFERS CROSSING. Every year treasure hunters dig happily up and down ELK CREEK seeking the rumored $60,000 in gold bullion buried by the "Reynolds Gang" many years ago after they robbed the stagecoach on RED HILL.

As you leave the village, the broad field to the right has a wonderful stand of leather flowers in June, their deep purple bells swaying in the breeze.

Left from SHAFFERS CROSSING is the side road leading to GLEN ELK, SPHINX PARK and PINE.

BAILEY, another early stage coach stop, is now a pleasant resort town.

SANTA MARIA was a popular summer resort called CASSELLS in the early days. Now it is famous for its beautiful white marble statue of CHRIST atop the nearby mountain.

At GRANT there is a picturesque dirt road leading right which angles cross

country to GEORGETOWN. Known as the GENEVA PARK TRAIL, this road for the off-the-beaten-track explorer, skirts MT. EVANS and MT. BIERSTADT. There is good fishing at GREEN and CLEAR LAKES.

Our By-Way tour continues through some dense forest of lodgepole pine, spruce and aspen. Then it tops a broad green saddleback called KENOSHA PASS where you will see one of the most exciting views in COLORADO. Stretched below is SOUTH PARK, a most prosaic name for what the early French trappers called BAYOU SALADO, meaning "salt marshes."

The broad flat park, about 60 miles long is rimmed with snow-capped mountains whose lower slopes are blanketed with pine and aspen forests making this a prime target for the shutter-bug who wants to get spectacular pictures of aspen gold in the autumn.

Our By-Way tour descends into SOUTH PARK to JEFFERSON. Today the meadows support fat cattle and several cuttings of the incomparable mountain hay are made each season.

There are two spectacular flower shows here each year. The first in late May and early June is when the blue iris bloom profusely. The second happens in August when the fringed gentian pinpoints the salt marshes with bright blue, truly a feast for the eyes.

At JEFFERSON there is a winding road to the left going southeast (State 77) paralleling the TARRYALL MOUNTAINS to TARRYALL and LAKE GEORGE. One of the last herds of mountain sheep in the state make their home in the nearby mountains.

You continue on U. S. 285 past COMO, once an important terminal on the narrow gauge railroad enroute to LEADVILLE. Just a mile off the highway, COMO is a semi-ghost town with the old hotel and railroad station still standing.

A delightful side trip may be taken here up over BOREAS PASS on the old narrow gauge roadbed which has been graded to handle auto traffic. A "must" for those who want the unusual side trip.

Highway 285 winds up and around RED HILL where the Reynolds gang robbed the stage so many years ago. Then it drops down to FAIRPLAY on the banks of the SOUTH PLATTE RIVER.

There are many interesting reminders here of the early days. Some of the gingerbread-trimmed Victorian houses still stand. The tiny picture-postcard Presbyterian Church built by Sheldon Jackson, "the missionary of all beyond," still serves the community.

The enterprising citizens of FAIRPLAY have restored many of the early buildings of the area so that the visitor can picture an early mining town as it was a hundred years ago.

A unique monument is one honoring PRUNES, a burro, who worked in most of the mines for many years.

From FAIRPLAY you follow State 9 to ALMA, once the richest gold mining camp in the country, and some mines are still being worked. The village owes most of its fame to a dancehall girl named SILVERHEELS who became an angel of mercy during a smallpox epidemic and nursed many of the villagers back to health. Afterwards she disappeared and many legends have grown up about her. The sparkling snow-capped mountain to the north is called MT. SILVERHEELS in her honor.

Just outside ALMA on a dirt road is the old cemetery where many of the smallpox victims were buried. The carving on many of the wooden markers is obliterated by time and weather. The fences, characteristic of these early ceme-

The O'Mailia

House

in Fairplay

teries, were built to keep out wild animals. Today the old cemetery is quiet and peaceful with aspen groves, red Indian paintbrush and blue columbines carpeting the graves.

About two miles beyond ALMA on the dirt road was BUCKSKIN JOE where H.A.W. Tabor ran a store before going to LEADVILLE where he made his millions in silver mining. Nearby in the stream bed are the remains of some Spanish *arrastres* used in the early days to crush the rock so the gold would settle to the bottom and be claimed. It is believed these *arrastres* were built by the Spaniards who came through here in the 1700's using Indian slaves to push the heavy stones. The miners made use of the *arrastres* in the 1800's using burros to grind the rock.

Our By-Way tour returns to State 9 at ALMA, turns left and climbs up over HOOSIER PASS named for all the "Hoosiers" who panned gold here in the early days. The peak to the right is MT. LINCOLN, named just before the president was assassinated.

The remains of an old mill near Alma

State 9 drops down into BRECKEN-RIDGE on the BLUE RIVER, one of the oldest and richest gold lode camps. Today it is a famous ski resort and much of the town has been restored. Good fishing and rockhounding is here in the summer and autumn.

The entire area between FAIRPLAY and BRECKENRIDGE is a rockhound's paradise. Old mine dumps, stream beds, slide rock, mountain ridges and placer beds yield such gemstones as topaz, tourmaline, turquoise, amethyst and garnets.

Our By-Way tour joins I 70 near FRISCO, a resort community made important by the construction of nearby DILLON DAM and RESERVOIR, with its resultant fishing and boating facilities. You turn right on I 70 past LAKE DILLON (RESERVOIR) to the SILVER-THORNE Exchange. Here you have a choice of two routes to complete your By-Way tour. One route follows I 70 which parallels STRAIGHT CREEK. Approximately six miles northeast you enter the West Portal of the famed EISENHOWER MEMORIAL TUNNEL completed in 1973. The tunnel runs under the CONTINENTAL DIVIDE for 1.7 miles and is called one of the "eight wonders of the world." At the East Portal you come out at the LOVELAND BASIN SKI AREA where U.S. 6 coming down off LOVELAND PASS joins I 70.

An alternate route and much more scenic (also longer) is to the right off SILVERTHORNE Exchange. Pick up U.S. 6 going past DILLON which was once located where the reservoir now stands. The town was moved to this new location when the dam was built. It is a popular boating, fishing and camping resort. Now the highway starts its long climb up over LOVELAND PASS considered by many persons to be the most dramatic and spectacular pass in COLORADO.

ARAPAHOE SKI BASIN, one of the best in the world for powder snow, is here with its ski lifts and smooth, treeless slopes.

The CONTINENTAL DIVIDE is crossed on LOVELAND PASS. The scenery is wonderful. The vast panorama stretched out below on either side is an awesome one. The peaks loom up jagged and blue.

The terrain is wind-swept and bare in many places. Dwarf willows hug the small

Historic photo of the Georgetown Loop ▶

Hotel

de Paris

in Georgetown

creeks of melted snow from nearby glaciers. Even during the summer there are snow banks in the deep ravines. Bright alpine flowers dot the mountainsides during the short summer season.

The road down from LOVELAND PASS is wide, but twisting and fairly steep. It drops down quickly to popular LOVELAND BASIN SKI AREA which is only about 50 miles west of DENVER. Here U.S. 6 joins I 70 again and continues past BROWNSVILLE.

SILVER PLUME is a semi-ghost town showing the ravages of time and weather on its Victorian buildings. There is still some mining nearby, but the village is primarily a resort area.

Leaving SILVER PLUME I 70 goes down CHUTE HILL, once a steep wagon road. To the right may be seen the old railroad grade and below the highway are the remnants of the once famous GEORGETOWN LOOP which was as well-known in the '80's and '90's as Niagara Falls, and visited by people from all over the world.

At the bottom of the canyon is the story book town of GEORGETOWN which looks like a Currier and Ives painting and is as Victorian as high button shoes. It is said by many persons to be the prettiest town in COLORADO.

There are many places of interest to visit here: the HOTEL DE PARIS (now a museum), the GRACE EPISCOPAL CHURCH, housing the oldest pipe organ in COLORADO still in use; the HAMILL HOUSE (also a museum); the COURTHOUSE built in 1866 and still used. The GEORGE MAXWELL HOUSE dominating the street above the Episcopal church was pictured in LIFE MAGAZINE as one of the ten outstanding examples of Victorian houses in America.

There are still three fire houses where the old fire equipment is kept.

The HOTEL DE PARIS is the most famous of the landmarks and was built by Louis Dupuy in architecture reminiscent of his birthplace, France. It was famed all over the country for its excellent cuisine. A fine china collection, a French library, diamond dust mirrors, and early Victorian decor are worth seeing.

West of the town is REPUBLICAN MOUNTAIN where, half way up, a rock-like figure stands as though leaving a rocky entrance. According to Indian legend, this represents an Indian maiden who was sacrificed for her people. The Ute Indians made annual pilgrimages here to visit this shrine. Today some persons refer to the figure as the VIRGIN and stories of tragedy have accumulated around those who try to climb to her.

The dirt road mentioned earlier as leaving GRANT (on U.S. 285) comes out here at GEORGETOWN.

Our By-Way tour now follows I 70 down CLEAR CREEK VALLEY to the junction with U.S. 40. This highway, leading to the left, goes up over BERTHOUD PASS to the WESTERN SLOPE of COLORADO. You follow I 70 east, skirting CLEAR CREEK and the towns of LAWSON, DUMONT and IDAHO SPRINGS to DENVER.

Colorado's Breadbasket

By-Way Tour No. 7

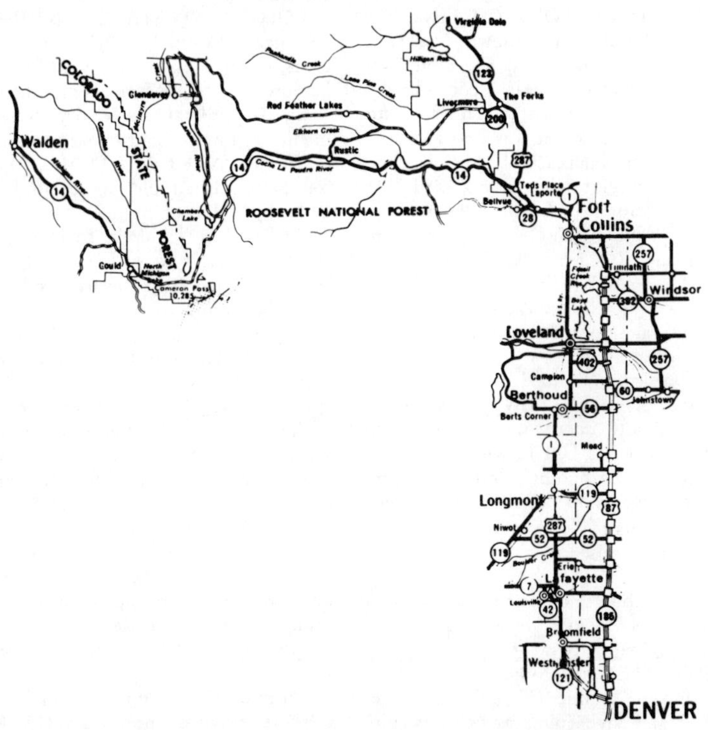

This By-Way tour takes you through tall, wide and handsome country, part of which is often called "Colorado's Breadbasket."

The road north from DENVER is one of the prettiest in the state because it gives wide vistas of plains, foothills and the gorgeous background of mountains, ever-changing in the light and shadow. It's truly a land of "purple mountain majesties above the fruited plain."

You should pick up U.S. 287 from DENVER going through BROOMFIELD which has boomed into an ideal suburban community. The view of the "Flatirons," the mountain ramparts near BOULDER, is excellent from this road. These "Flatirons" are huge, uptilted granite slabs rearing picturesquely along the foothills south of the city.

A By-Way tour west from the highway on State 170, eleven miles, takes you to ELDORADO SPRINGS at the mouth of SOUTH BOULDER CANYON. One of the earliest resorts in the state, there is excellent swimming, hiking and horseback riding here.

Return to U.S. 287 to LAFAYETTE, center of a once prosperous coal mining area. The land above the ground is not only fertile, but the entire region beneath the ground is honeycombed with tunnels.

Old mine dumps dot the landscape with their yellow, red and brown tailings.

LONGMONT was a planned community, divided into small tracts and sold to farmers in 1870. It was named for nearby LONGS PEAK which dominates the area. The small city is considered one of the gateways to ESTES and ROCKY MOUN-

TAIN NATIONAL PARK. The first ore mill brought to Boulder County in 1859 still stands at 4th and Kimbark streets. It's made of a granite block with a large cavity to hold the ore and an outlet for the pulverized rock, a crude mortar-type mill.

The countryside between LONGMONT, LOVELAND and FORT COLLINS is a rich agricultural district showing fields of sugar beets, pinto beans, vegetables for canning — tomatoes, peas, cucumbers — alfalfa and dryland wheat. The seed for this hard winter wheat was brought originally in their knapsacks by the Russian-German immigrants in the '80's and '90's when they came to tend the beet fields.

LOVELAND, another gateway to ESTES and ROCKY MOUNTAIN NATIONAL PARK, has become well-known as the "Sweetheart City" because so many valentines are mailed from here on Valentine's Day.

The city was named for W. A. H. Loveland, one of the early railroad builders. Originally there was a settlement nearby called ST. LOUIS which had been founded by disappointed miners returning from the gold fields. These miners-turned-farmers made so much money from the food they raised that they settled down to stay.

The St. Louis Hotel and Stage Station on St. Louis Avenue are all that remain of the original settlement.

LOVELAND PIONEER MUSEUM, 503 Lincoln Avenue (U. S. 287), houses mineral and archaeological exhibits, pioneer and Indian artifacts, and a fine gun collection. The museum is a pioneer residence.

Between here and FORT COLLINS are hundreds of acres of cherry and apple orchards which perfume the air for miles and look like a sea of pink in the spring.

The red-black Montmorency is the favorite cherry raised, and cherry and apple cider is a delightful beverage sold here.

FORT COLLINS is a prosperous farming and trading center founded in 1864 on orders from President Abraham Lincoln as a military post to protect early travelers.

COLORADO STATE UNIVERSITY (formerly Colorado A&M) has a spacious, lovely campus. It is world-renowned because of its modern approach in the fields of animal husbandry, veterinary medicine, forestry and home economics.

The PIONEER MUSEUM, 219 Peterson Street, is an old log cabin built in 1844 by a French trapper, Antoine Jannis, first white settler in Larimer County. It contains a fine collection of ancient Indian artifacts found nearby and pioneer relics belonging to early settlers.

Continuing on U. S. 287, we pass TERRY LAKE, surrounded by cherry and apple orchards, a lovely sight in the spring. LINDEMEIR SITE, north of the highway, is one of the most important archeological sites in the world. Permission must be obtained to dig here for arrowheads and other artifacts, many of which belonged to Folsom man.

LAPORTE is one of the oldest villages in the state, having been founded in 1860 on the site of an old French-Canadian trading post. At one time they considered putting the capital of Colorado Territory here.

An interesting side trip leaves U. S. 287 a short distance out of LAPORTE and goes west through BELLVUE following RIST CANYON, once a frontier toll road.

The EARLY TRAPPERS MONUMENT on the grounds of a roadside country house marks the approximate site where a party of French trappers were caught in a snowstorm in 1836. They

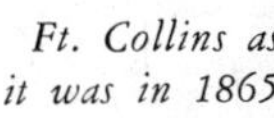

Ft. Collins as it was in 1865

"cached" their supplies here and in the spring returned to find them intact. Hence they called the river "Cache La Poudre."

The well-graveled road winds through RIST CANYON and climbs to the top of STOVE PRAIRIE HILL. A road to the left leaves the highway and you climb BUCK-HORN MOUNTAIN. From the top is a sweeping panorama of the Rockies to the west and the high plains to the east. You gaze down on checkerboard-like fields of the fertile POUDRE VALLEY interlaced by irrigation canals.

You may continue north past Stove Prairie School to the POUDRE CANYON road, or go back to U. S. 287.

Next is TED'S PLACE where we leave U. S. 287 and follow "Colorado's Trout Route" up the Poudre River. Here is some of the finest trout fishing in the state.

This picturesque canyon road winds through LITTLE NARROWS with its red granite walls hung with green and yellow lichen and scrawny pine trees clinging precariously to the rocky ledges.

You are now in ROOSEVELT NA-TIONAL FOREST and soon the trees become more dense. FORT COLLINS MOUNTAIN PARK, owned by the city, has a lovely hiking trail marking every variety of tree and mountain flower native to the vicinity.

A couple of miles past RUSTIC is a road leading to the right up PINGREE HILL whose steep sides are scarred with abandoned prospect holes and mine shafts. A good place for the rockhound to look for specimen. This road joins one on

Columbines, the State Flower

which MANHATTAN, a ghost town of deserted log cabins, is located.

Our By-Way tour skirts CHAMBERS LAKE, lying blue and cold where the LARAMIE RIVER heads. At the forks in the road, another By-Way tour would take you south over CAMERON PASS, then west and north to WALDEN in NORTH PARK, whose backroads lead to unexcelled fishing and hunting.

At the forks, you turn north abruptly, following the LARAMIE RIVER to NEW and OLD GLENDEVEY, right in the lap of nature. To the west is the vast RA-WAH PRIMITIVE AREA where the U. S. Forest Service forbids construction of cabins, roads and other "blemishes of civilization." Wild, awe-inspiring, rugged, this is truly primeval country left as it was before the coming of the white man.

A big part of the area's charm comes from the unspoiled attraction that Nature provides for those who would escape the hustle and bustle of city life. Here the fisherman, the picnicker, the camper, the hiker, and those who like to take pack trips will find excellent facilities.

The mighty Rockies—the MUMMY RANGE to the south, the RAWAHS of the MEDICINE BOW RANGE to the west, and the SNOWY RANGE (in Wyoming to the north) stand out in bold beauty against the skyline. Some of the most beautiful beds of blue columbine, COLORADO'S state flower, are found in the aspen groves in this vicinity.

If you really like to get off-the-beaten-path and explore back country roads, take the middle fork of the road seven miles north of OLD GLENDEVEY. This route winds through wild and primeval country past CHIMNEY ROCK, an early landmark, and eventually into TIE SIDING in WYOMING (U. S. 287). This is really lonely country with only an occasional sheepherder's wagon and many flocks of sheep on summer pasture.

On this route you return via U. S. 287. The road swings southeast through rolling foothills broken by grotesque masses of sandstone. The VIRGINIA DALE MONUMENT points the way to the old Virginia Dale Station on the OVER-LAND STAGE. It was established in 1862 when the OVERLAND was forced by Indian depradations to operate through COLORADO, and was named for "Jack" Slade's wife—he was the notorious killer of Jules Beni of JULESBURG.

A view of Ft. Lupton built around 1836

South of VIRGINIA DALE, the highway traverses rolling country, crosses several creeks that are dry ravines most of the year, and penetrates more rugged country.

At THE FORKS, U. S. 287 meets one other route back from OLD GLENDEVEY. This By-Way tour takes the right hand fork seven miles north of OLD GLENDEVEY, and swings southeast about 17 miles to RED FEATHER LAKES. Enroute you will pass DEADMAN MOUNTAIN. Atop is the U. S. Forest fire lookout tower where you may join the "Squirrel Club" if you climb to the top.

At RED FEATHER LAKES you may live in the kind of world vacation daydreams are made of—fishing, swimming, remoteness, boating, doing nothing and blue, blue water. There are ten lakes here —two of them open to public fishing— TWIN and DOWDY.

From RED FEATHER LAKES there are alternate roads back to U. S. 287. A country road south to MANHATTAN, a ghost town mentioned earlier, and site of another Ranger Station. They will direct you to a foot trail leading to a pinon grove which is one of the most northerly growths of this tree in America. The age of some of the pinons has been fixed at 4000 years, about the same as that of the California redwoods. Many of the pinons are four feet in diameter, largest specimen known. Follow the road east about six miles to LOG CABIN.

Another By-Way from RED FEATHER LAKES is the road leading southeast 8 miles to LOG CABIN, thence through LIVERMORE to THE FORKS on U. S. 287.

LIVERMORE was built in 1863 by Adolph Livernash and Stephen Moore as a cattle ranch.

A third By-Way from RED FEATHER LAKES is northeast via CHEROKEE PARK (16 miles), then southeast 12 miles to U. S. 287 (about three miles north of THE FORKS). Spring Hill Ranch is a mile from the junction.

Our By-Way tour returns to U. S. 287 and goes south through OWL CANYON, twisting between limestone cliffs that wall the narrow gorge. You follow the highway to FORT COLLINS turning left (east) on State 14 for nine miles, then south on State 257 to WINDSOR which is another prosperous farming community.

Another six miles and State 257 joins U. S. 34 where our By-Way tour turns east to GREELEY, center of one of the richest agricultural sections in the state and founded in 1870 by Nathan C. Meeker, agricultural editor of the NEW YORK TRIBUNE.

Although first known as the UNION COLONY, the town was later named after the editor of the TRIBUNE, Horace Greeley, who popularized the phrase, "Go West, young man, go West!" Early potatoes and Greeley "wonder" melons have made the area famous.

Important places of interest in the lovely little tree-shaded town are the COLORADO STATE COLLEGE (U. S. 85 & 34), the old WELD COUNTY JAIL at the rear of the Courthouse (9th Street and 9th Avenue), and the MEEKER MEMORIAL MUSEUM, 1324 Ninth Avenue.

U. S. 85 goes southwest through LA SALLE and GILCREST, two farming communities, through PLATTEVILLE to FORT VASQUEZ which has been restored. Built in 1836 by Louis Vasquez and Andrew Sublette, mountain men and fur traders, it was a crossroad and rendezvous of voyageurs till the end of the fur days.

FORT LUPTON was originally a trading post built in 1836 by Lancaster P. Lupton and a marker tells that it was the first permanent settlement in northern COLORADO.

BRIGHTON, another farming community, is one of the largest sugar beet centers in the state. U. S. 85 now takes you 20 miles to DENVER.

PART 2

TABLE OF CONTENTS

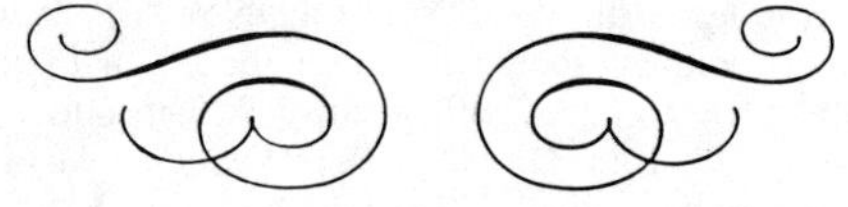

COLORADO

Pikes Peak

This southeastern section of COLORADO has its own particular charm and flavor, and is different in many ways from the other parts of the state. Here is felt the influence of the Spanish conquistadores who came in the 16th Century and left their imprint on the people, the names, the customs and a way of life. The farther south you travel in the state, the more aware you are of this influence.

Even the name COLORADO is a Spanish one meaning "red." This particular area emphasizes that color in its rocks, canyons, water and the chili peppers which decorate tiny adobe houses in the SAN LUIS VALLEY. SPANISH PEAKS and the SANGRE DE CRISTO RANGE (Blood of Christ) dominate the southern half of the area. Spanish names such as La Junta, Las Animas, Pueblo, La Veta and San Luis outnumber the Anglo names. El Rio de Las Animas Perdidas en Purgatorio (River of the Souls Lost in Purgatory) which runs through TRINIDAD was corrupted by the French trappers to PURGATOIRE, and further corrupted by the cowboys to "Picketwire." You'll hear it called both names today.

PIKES PEAK, the great mountain which stands out from the ROCKIES like a sentinel, has an aura all its own and dominates the upper half of this area both physically and emotionally. It's an ever changing picture of strength, grandeur and beauty. Sometimes it stands clear as an etching — other times it's encircled with lazily rolling fleecy clouds.

Reaching 14,110 feet into the cool blue sky, it was seen a hundred miles away by Lt. Zebulon Pike and his party when they came in 1806 to survey the boundaries of the newly purchased Louisiana Territory.

Lt. Pike maintained it would never be climbed by mortal man, but he's been proved wrong thousands of times. Today in addition to hiking and burro trails, a cog railway and an automobile road take visitors to the summit.

This part of COLORADO is a good place to live, to work, to play, and to visit. You may choose a variety of vacations. Practically any kind you name is there for the asking — hiking, horseback riding, fishing, swimming, camping, boating, rock-hounding, taking pictures — you name it and southern COLORADO will offer it to you.

Colorado Springs Area

By-Way Tour No. 1

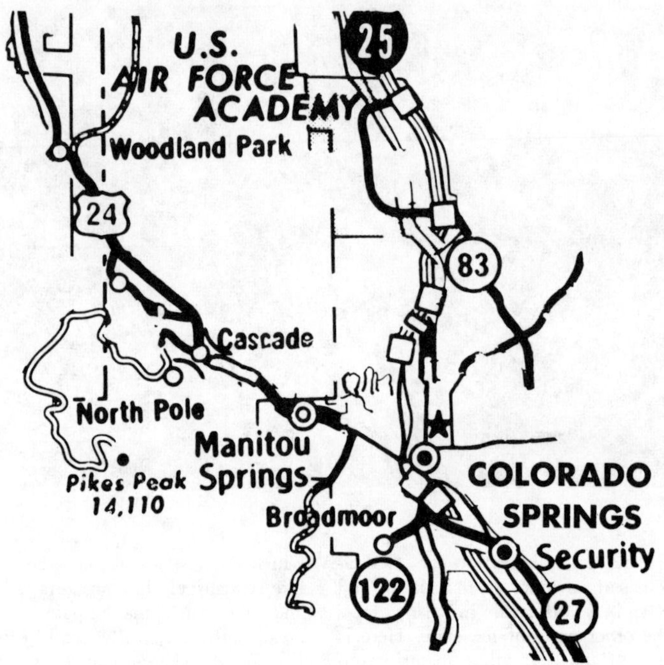

COLORADO SPRINGS at the foot of PIKES PEAK is a city of wide streets, handsome homes, exclusive society, a cultural center, and the base of NORAD, nerve center of the North American Air Defense Command. It has been a top tourist lure for three-quarters of a century.

Familiarly known as "Little Lunnon" because so many young Englishmen came after its founding in 1871, the city still has an international flavor. General William Jackson Palmer, who built the DENVER & RIO GRANDE RAILROAD, bought the land where the city now stands and laid out the town site.

He also helped found COLORADO COLLEGE whose tree-shaded campus is directly north of the business district. Beautiful SHOVE CHAPEL dominates the campus.

Nearby the FINE ARTS CENTER, 18 West Dale, is hub for many of the cultural activities of the city. They have a superior art collection and an enviable array of early Spanish-American religious art indigenous to southern COLORADO and New Mexico.

The CITY MUSEUM, 25 West Kiowa Street, has excellent historical and archeological displays. MONUMENT VALLEY PARK, extending two and one-half miles along MONUMENT CREEK, is a picturesque spot for picnics and recreation.

Visitors are welcome at the VAN BRIGGLE ART POTTERY, 1125 Glen Avenue, where world-famous pottery is made.

The real lure of COLORADO SPRINGS, though, is in the varied scenic and historic sites that surround it. The city is like a corridor from which doors open to a host of different attractions.

Synonymous with COLORADO SPRINGS is the world-renowned

BROADMOOR HOTEL. Leave downtown COLORADO SPRINGS on U. S. 85 & 87 and cross FOUNTAIN CREEK. Turn right on any one of the four marked avenues which lead through the beautiful BROADMOOR area with its palatial homes.

The hotel itself is silhouetted majestically against the mountains. Here are entertained the great and the near-great who visit the city and state. The grounds are beautifully landscaped, and all types of recreation are available.

Several delightful side trips may be made from here. One goes south past the golf course and up CHEYENNE MOUNTAIN to one of the finest zoos (fee) in the country. Beyond is the WILL ROGERS SHRINE OF THE SUN with its melodious carillon chimes. The road snakes its way to the top of CHEYENNE MOUNTAIN to a lodge where spectacular views of the entire area may be seen.

Another By-Way tour goes up CHEYENNE CANYON (toll) to SEVEN FALLS, as beautiful at night as in the daytime because of the stunning lighting effects.

The NORTH CHEYENNE CANYON road goes through a lovely woodsy canyon leading eventually into a beautiful red rock canyon studded with green pines and juniper. At BRUIN INN State 336 turns left and becomes the thrilling GOLD CAMP ROAD twisting and turning through breathtaking scenery and terrain to CRIPPLE CREEK.

Our By-Way tour picks up State 336 and turns right continuing northeast on the old railroad bed, hugging the red mountainside, zipping through tunnels, and hanging on sheer cliffs looking down thousands of feet below on BROADMOOR and COLORADO SPRINGS.

This road eventually meets U. S. 24 (Colorado Avenue) in west COLORADO SPRINGS. Nearby is GHOST TOWN, a well-restored western village. Turn left on U. S. 24 until you see a sign saying "GARDEN OF THE GODS."

Turn right and in less than a mile you enter that fascinating red sandstone wonderland with its green juniper trees which were young when Columbus discovered America. BALANCED ROCK, STEAMBOAT ROCK, CHIEF MANITOU, HIDDEN INN and other landmarks are there for your pleasure. The camera enthusiast will love it, particularly near sunrise or sunset when the sun brings out its most striking colors.

Back to U. S. 24, then you drive into MANITOU SPRINGS, a famous spa and pleasure resort, at the foot of PIKES PEAK. Named by the Utes for their "Great Spirit," it was used for centuries by the Indians who bathed in its healing waters.

Adjacent to the town and up PHANTOM CANYON are the CLIFF DWELLINGS (fee) which show how the Indians lived hundreds of years ago. Then you may take a scenic and thrilling trip to the CAVE OF THE WINDS (fee) which contains a fairyland of stalactites and stalagmites.

A short side trip to CRYSTAL PARK (toll) south of MANITOU leads to CAMERON CONE, a good place for the rockhound to find nice specimen of smoky quartz, rock crystal, yellow phenakite, pinkish topaz and lovely blue-green amazonstones which resemble turquoise. In fact, this whole PIKES PEAK area is known as one of the finest places in the world to find gem stones.

The MANITOU AND PIKES PEAK COG RAILROAD, highest scenic moun-

Balanced Rock in Garden of the Gods

tain cog railroad in the world, is an exciting way to reach the summit of the mighty peak. It's hard for words to describe the varied scenes enroute. There are foot and burro trails for the hardy and adventurous of spirit who want to climb the peak.

To climb PIKES PEAK in your auto follow U.S. 26 west from MANITOU over UTE PASS to CASCADE, a well-known summer resort. Take the left hand marked road and start up the highway past SANTA'S WORKSHOP, a "must" for the children. The road ascends rapidly via wide switchbacks to OBSERVATION POINT.

Here you gaze below into endless wilderness of yellow and Ponderosa pine, green and blue spruce, and Douglas fir. The "young" forest of fir trees en route was planted some years ago to cover the burn caused by a forest fire which the warring Utes started many years before the white man came.

Blue harebells, purple monkshood, lavender columbine, and yellow pea flowers carpet the forest floor during summer. Near timberline brilliant mountain pinks, purple gentian and blue forget-me-nots appear between the rocks and clumps of tundra. Gnarled, crooked pines, fighting for their existence against the great odds of wind and weather, are silhouetted against the sky.

Thrilling glimpses in every direction follow you up the road. At ELK PARK is a favorite ski resort. On the 4th of July there is an annual auto race where daredevils race up to a hundred miles an hour around these hairpin curves.

At the summit you are literally "on top of the world." You will look at this drama of stone and weather and wonder if the slow process of geological architecture ever fashioned anything more fitting. Awesome vistas stretch in every direction and encompass many mountain ranges, tall peaks, jewel-like lakes and upland meadows.

To the south are the SANGRE DE CRISTOS and the SPANISH PEAKS rising in majestic beauty. To the west is the CONTINENTAL DIVIDE barricading the blue horizon. To the north are MOUNT EVANS and LONGS PEAK, whose crests of shimmering white glaciers look like giant ice cream cones just out of reach. To the east is COLORADO SPRINGS, beyond is BLACK FOREST, and finally the HIGH PLAINS.

An exciting sight is to stand among the weather-shattered rocks at the summit and watch the cog railway laboriously clunk its way up the mountain as it has for more than 60 years.

The wind blows a gale most of the time at the summit. You'll probably be pelted with some rain or hail — it might even snow, even in the middle of the summer, if a cloud drifts across the peak. After all, you're 14,110 feet up in the clouds.

Many persons plan their trip to see the sun rise or set from the summit because of its breathtaking beauty. The trip down is as thrilling as the trip up with many sights to see.

COLORADO SPRINGS is a center for the Armed Services claiming FORT CARSON, ENT AIR FORCE BASE and PETERSON FIELD. A By-Way tour to the north ten miles via Interstate 25 leads to the AIR FORCE ACADEMY covering 17,800 acres of wooded slopes at the base of RAMPART RANGE. For its main buildings, the ACADEMY combines glass, steel, aluminum and colored tile in a stunning composition of contemporary design.

On the return trip to COLORADO SPRINGS leave Interstate 25 at the WOODMAN ROAD exit. This partially-paved and well-graded country road winds among mushroom-shaped rocks to a monastary, then turns south. In the spring you may see flocks of bluebirds which have wintered in the sheltered canyons.

You will pass Glen Eyrie on the right, built by William Jackson Palmer as his home. It is now owned by a religious organization.

At the next fork in the road, take the left one which climbs abruptly to the top of a mesa. Below, the other road joins the east entrance to the GARDEN OF THE GODS. You'll pass the handsome GARDEN OF THE GODS CLUB built to take full advantage of its priceless view of PIKES PEAK and the GARDEN OF THE GODS.

This is MESA ROAD leading through a lovely new residential district, dropping down to MONUMENT CREEK and finally into COLORADO SPRINGS proper.

◀ *The United States Air Force Academy*

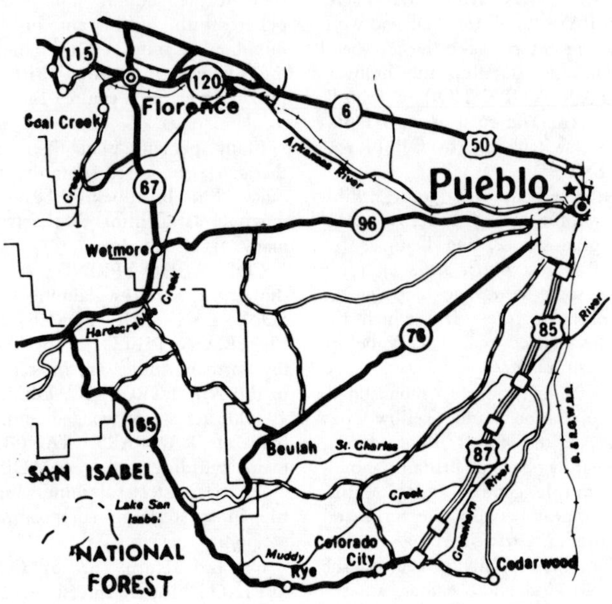

PUEBLO is often called "little Pittsburgh" because of its steel mills which color the sky with pink, yellow and gray smoke plumes. The second largest city in the state, it is truly a "melting pot" because over the years people have come from many lands to work in the mills — Italians, Slavs, Czechoslovakians, Poles, Danes, Austrians, and Spanish-Americans.

As the city has grown and prospered, it has become a thriving manufacturing center with many fine homes to show the standard of living.

PUEBLO'S history dates back many years. Some evidence has been found that the early Spanish explorers camped here at the confluence of the ARKANSAS and FOUNTAIN rivers as early as the 16th or 17th Centuries.

French fur traders were here in 1761. In 1806 Lt. Pike and his party were the first Americans to erect a structure here, a three-sided log stockade. Kit Carson, Dick Wootten and other mountain men came through on the Trapper's Trail between Fort Laramie and Santa Fe, building their campfires under "Old Monarch," a venerable cottonwood which was cut down in 1882.

Jim Beckwourth, another trader, is credited with building "El Pueblo," a square adobe fort which General Fremont and Parkman both mention in their diaries. A party of Mormons spent the winter of 1846 here, and during the gold rush of 1858-9 many persons came through enroute to the "diggin's."

But it wasn't until William J. Palmer pushed the DENVER & RIO GRANDE RAILROAD through in 1872 that the young town really began to grow. The COLORADO FUEL AND IRON CORPORATION, built in 1881 (also promoted by Palmer), brought prosperity and the city grew by leaps and bounds.

The phenomenal growth of agriculture in the ARKANSAS VALLEY to the east has contributed to PUEBLO'S economic stability. It has become a tourist center because of its accessibility to the various mountain and recreation areas directly to the west within 30 or 40 minutes drive.

EL PUEBLO MUSEUM is an interesting place to visit. The COLORADO FUEL AND IRON MILLS (tours) in the south part of the city called BESSEMER have a peculiar fascination at night when their mighty furnaces, stacks and slag piles paint the sky a fiery red.

The COLORADO STATE FAIR GROUNDS, Summit and Beulah avenues, play host to the State Fair in late August. There are over 200 acres of city parks, a well-maintained zoo and many picnic areas.

On leaving PUEBLO, our By-Way tour follows U.S. 50 northwest across wide rolling grasslands with dramatic stands of branched cacti which have bright red flowers in the early summer.

About 18 miles west a country road turns right to STONE CITY. Here large limestone quarries and the petrified skeleton of Tyrannosauras Rex, a giant dinosaur, are seen. There is good hunting here for fossils.

As you continue west on U.S. 50, low rolling hills appear covered with pinon pine and juniper. Turn left on State 120 which takes you through PORTLAND named for the huge cement factories.

Fruit orchards appear on either side of the road leading into FLORENCE which celebrates an annual Apple Blossom Day. Jesse Frazier, a pioneer who brought the seedlings from Missouri, planted the first apple orchard. He also opened the first coal mines nearby which were important in the area's early development.

The second oldest oil well in the United States was drilled in 1876 near FLORENCE. It's a freak formation where geologists say no oil should exist. However, the Indians had used the oil scum which formed on ponds for medicinal purposes before the white man came. A. M. Cassidy drilled the first well and hauled oil by the barrel to PUEBLO, DENVER and SANTA FE.

An interesting side trip up COAL CREEK CANYON shows where the bones of a 20-foot Stegosaurus were found in the sandstone. Petrified bones are found in the cuts and canyons. Brick foundations, rusting machinery and tumbledown shacks show where a large gold reduction mill once stood. It handled the entire output of CRIPPLE CREEK in the boom days, but fire and labor troubles finally closed the mill. Numerous coal mines dot the mountainsides, mostly one or two-man operations.

This road ends at State 67 and our By-Way tour goes south to WETMORE, once a stagecoach station, set in a beautiful forest of conifers. A few weathered frame buildings rub shoulders with cabins built by summer residents. You are now in the WET MOUNTAINS, so named by the Mormon pioneers in 1846; after crossing the plains they were delighted to see heavy rain clouds hanging on the peaks of this range.

The road now follows HARD-SCRABBLE CREEK past KIT CARSON ROCK where the well-known scout carved his and his wife's initials. This is known as the KIT CARSON TRAIL because he and other mountain men used it when they went hunting in the WET MOUNTAIN VALLEY beyond. Explorer John C. Fremont followed this route seeking a direct passage for a railroad to the Pacific coast.

As you climb the steep canyon road you enter SAN ISABEL NATIONAL FOREST. Beautiful stands of blue spruce, Ponderosa and white pine, and fir cover the hillsides. Pink and purple penstemon, blue larkspur, red Indian paint brush, and tiny yellow sunflowers cover sunny slopes during the summer. As you top a rise you get a dramatic view of the SANGRE DE CRISTOS (Blood of Christ).

Our By-Way tour turns south at MCKENZIE on State 76 following BIGELOW CREEK through lovely Ponderosa pine forests.

A short hike up OPHIR CREEK to the right takes you to a ghost mining camp, OPHIR, where the rockhounds can find good specimen. The fisherman will find excellent trout fishing in the beaver dams along this creek.

Back on State 76 to FAIRVIEW, you go through Davenport Gulch filled with unusually large aspen trees to DAVENPORT picnic grounds.

You may continue on State 76 northeast to PUEBLO via BEULAH. This route is discussed later.

Our road picks up State 165 at DAVENPORT, climbs GREENHILL DIVIDE and drops down Willow Creek to SAN ISABEL RECREATION AREA and ice-blue LAKE ISABEL. Here is paradise for the trout fisherman. Horseback and hiking trails abound. Pack trips take you into the WET MOUNTAINS which are crisscrossed with creeks and gulches with such interesting names as Revelie, Deerlick, Lipan, Janes' Gulch, Hatchet, and Gobler's Knob. For the hunter, deer, elk, mountain sheep, antelope, wild turkeys, and grouse are plentiful in season.

Right from LAKE ISABEL is a country road leading to MARION MINE and lake. Good ore specimen are found on the dumps.

Our tour follows State 165 through the Canyon of the Muddy Creek with its fantastically carved walls and caves which are fun to explore. RYE is another summer resort and pack trip supply area.

Right from RYE is a country road leading to GREENHORN MOUNTAIN, named for a famous Comanche chief, CUERNO VERDE, who was chased up here from New Mexico by the Spanish General DeVaca and killed.

State 165 swings northeast to I 25 through a new town called COLORADO CITY. Nearby is the HICKLIN RANCH, named for Alex Hicklin who came here in 1846 with General Kearny's army during the Mexican War.

Our By-Way tour continues 27 miles north, passes beautiful LAKE MINNEQUA to PUEBLO.

Another By-Way tour, which is a little shorter, may be taken from PUEBLO. It is a circle within the circle we have just explored.

This time you leave PUEBLO on State 76 going southwest across BOGG'S FLATS, a series of low hogbacks pinpointed with scrub juniper. Huge cattle roundups were held here in the early days.

MULDOON HILL was the site of a hoax many years ago. A Mr. Conant claimed he discovered a giant figure in the canyons supposed to be the body of a prehistoric man. Conant is supposed to have refused $20,000 from P. T. Barnum to exhibit it. A Yale professor uncovered the fraud.

The terrain changes now, as the road begins to climb slightly. Scrub oak which turns a beautiful red in the autumn is

An old abandoned blacksmith shop

Action at the Colorado State Fair

abundant. Snow-on-the-mountain, a lovely green and white flower, grows in large patches.

GOODPASTURE is next. To the south was the famous Three R Ranch whose feudal life was described in HARPER'S MAGAZINE in 1878. Indian petroglyphs may be seen on the rocky walls of nearby St. Charles River.

State 76 skirts SIGNAL HILL first used by the Indians. Later the government flashed warnings of Indian raids from here to PIKES PEAK to the north and SPANISH PEAKS to the south. This area was known as MACE'S HOLE and during the Civil War Federal troops drove out Confederate sympathizers who had gathered here.

Off the highway to the right about two miles is BEULAH, a center of a large marble deposit. The beautiful onyx used in the interior of the STATE CAPITOL in DENVER was quarried here. Interesting mineral specimen may be found. Today BEULAH is primarily a resort town although many persons live here the year around and drive to work every day in PUEBLO.

PUEBLO MUNICIPAL CAMPGROUND, owned by the city, has many fine facilities for vacationists. Hiking and horseback trails abound. Drive on west here through Squirrel Creek Drive to DAVENPORT PICNIC GROUNDS. Here you turn north (right) on State 274, a short by-pass, crossing three Hardscrabble Creeks, joining State 96.

At WETMORE, you turn right again (east) and follow State 96, the same route followed by Lt. Pike in 1806. You begin to drop down now out of the mountains across prairie covered with buffalo grass with grain and alfalfa fields along the river. GOODNIGHT is named for the old GOODNIGHT RANCH which was once owned by Colonel Charles Goodnight who drove Texas longhorns up here over the GOODNIGHT TRAIL from Texas.

State 96 ends at PUEBLO.

Rampart Range and Platte Canyon

By-Way Tour No. 3

The RAMPART RANGE ROAD, a scenic drive between COLORADO SPRINGS and DENVER, is a "must" for those who like "off-the-beaten path" routes. Much of it isn't even paved, but the roads are graveled and well-graded.

Our By-Way tour leaves COLORADO SPRINGS via U. S. 24 to MANITOU SPRINGS, turning north through the GARDEN OF THE GODS. At the northwest edge of this colorful playground, a road takes off uphill. Winding and twisting on breathtaking switchbacks, the road affords a sweeping panorama of the entire COLORADO SPRINGS area.

Finally you enter PIKE NATIONAL FOREST with its beautiful stands of Douglas fir and Englemann spruce highlighted by lighter green aspen groves.

Beaver dams reflecting the blue sky stud the creeks. Ferny glens along the meandering creek appeal to the camper and picnicker. In the early spring purple arbutus peek from beneath matted pine needles, followed by blue chiming bells, scarlet Indian paint brush and pink fairy trumpets.

The road is thickly forested in most places with some areas showing timber cuts. Now the highway cuts wide swaths around the canyon, climbing until great outcroppings of pink Pikes Peak granite appear on every side. VIRGIN'S BATH CAMP GROUND, named for the huge bathtub-like rock which dominates the mountainside, is a good place to stop. Off to the south and west are splendid views of the huge rocks which guard the SOUTH PLATTE RIVER CANYON.

To the east about a half mile is a ridge above a small meadow which is a rockhound's paradise. Here some of the finest specimen of clear and yellow topaz have been found in Colorado, as well as smoky quartz in rock crystal.

About one-half mile south of VIR-GIN'S BATH is WHITE QUARTZ MOUNTAIN (to the right), another good place to find both smoky and clear quartz crystals. Stream beds and gulleys throughout the area have yielded good specimens.

Back on the highway you drive north to a junction marked "DEVIL'S HEAD." Turn right and follow a winding road to DEVIL'S HEAD CAMP GROUND, a delightful place to picnic and hike along marked trails. Huge rocks tower above a cozy glen, almost encircling it. Stately pine and tall aspen trees give it a leafy, restful atmosphere.

DEVIL'S HEAD LOOKOUT STA-TION crowns the peak sitting like a rakish hat on the brow of the mountain. For the stout of heart, lung and limb, the steep mile-long hike almost straight up to the station is worth the effort.

From here and SQUAW MOUNTAIN LOOKOUT STATION to the northwest the rangers can easily spot tell-tale fire smoke. The view in every direction is sublime.

Our By-Way tour leaves DEVIL'S HEAD and returns to the main road which now straightens out somewhat and follows the backbone of a high ridge. This is RAMPART RANGE which is the first range of mountains separating the foothills from the higher Rockies.

To the east are the rolling foothills cut by streams, then the BLACK FOREST and finally the high plains extending east into Kansas. To the west are dramatic vistas of parallel ranges separated by deep canyons. Each range rises a little higher until the CONTINENTAL DIVIDE cuts the blue sky, its white snow crown dazzling in the sun.

There are lookout points along the road where a short pause will let you feast your eyes on panoramas filled with broken jumbled country, mountain peaks, rugged timbered slopes, and a blue haze shrouding the canyons.

To the northwest is lofty MOUNT EVANS dominating the skyline. To the west is the PARK RANGE, north and west of FAIRPLAY. Looking back you get a close-up of spectacular DEVIL'S HEAD, a jutting mass of red Pikes Peak granite upthrust in lonely isolation.

The sights from this road are stunning any time of day or year. Some mornings the mists rise from the SOUTH PLATTE RIVER like soft white veils. At sunset, the sky is a riot of color with deep purple and blue haze hanging in the valleys.

After the first snow the spruce and pine trees look as though they'd been dusted with powdered sugar. And in the fall gay yellows, orange and reds highlight the aspen and scrub oak.

A few miles north of DEVIL'S HEAD watch for an unmarked road leading to the right. For the brave soul interested in a thrilling old-time mountain road, take this one (one-way part of the time) to PERRY PARK (State 105). It's a few short miles, but the road drops rapidly about 2,000 feet around steep, breath-taking switchbacks.

Our By-Way tour continues on the RAMPART RANGE Road until it joins State 67.

To the right ten miles is SEDALIA (U. S. 85) through showy JARRE CAN-YON. This heavily wooded canyon drops abruptly with wide hairpin curves giving glimpses from time to time of the peaks to the west and the plains to the east.

You turn left on State 67 through lovely forested regions and mountain meadows, then angle down quickly to DECKERS on the south fork of the SOUTH PLATTE RIVER.

This resort village caters to fishermen, picnickers, hikers and campers. Dude

Climbing to the Devil's Head Lookout Tower

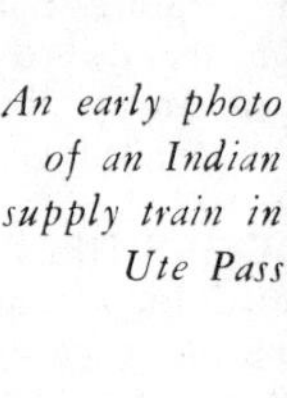

An early photo of an Indian supply train in Ute Pass

ranches abound. DECKERS makes a nice hub from which to fan out and explore a number of back country roads. It's a country where you can spend a day or a week or a month exploring, fishing, swimming, or just plain resting.

One road will take you to picturesque CHEESMAN DAM, named for the engineer-organizer of DENVER'S water system, one of the sources of DENVER'S water supply.

Another delightful place is WELLINGTON LAKE. "Red Rock Castle" is seen across the lake against the TARRY-ALL MOUNTAINS. This road leads through ESTABROOK to BAILEY on U. S. 285.

A really "off-the-beaten-path" road follows the SOUTH PLATTE RIVER down stream for several miles, then curves around a bend to BUFFALO CREEK, another resort village.

The better known route to BUFFALO CREEK, however, (and equally scenic) follows State 126 north and west to the village, then to PINE and to SHAFFERS CROSSING (U. S. 285).

But a "must see" place is a little side road between PINE and GLEN ELK called SPHINX PARK. A more twisted, jumbled region of rocks would be hard to find. Tumbled rocky escarpments wall the narrow valley. A sphinx-like rock guards the place. Year-round homes and summer cottages cling precariously to the almost vertical sides of the canyon.

Beyond it's just a few miles through GLEN ELK to SHAFFERS CROSSING where it's less than forty miles to DENVER via U. S. 285.

To return to COLORADO SPRINGS our By-Way tour takes off southeast on a good paved road from DECKERS to WESTLAKE and WOODLAND PARK. This road parallels the RAMPART RANGE road except now you skirt small creeks and wide canyons.

Along the winding road from early spring until late fall, mountain flowers bloom in abundance, especially after a wet spring. Azure larkspur, red fringed Indian paint brush, blue beardstongue, and golden banner brighten the hillsides early. Later there are fine shows of purple aster, orange gaillardias, yellow narrowleaf sunflowers, red loco, dainty blue harebells, tall green gentians and white miner's candles.

You'll see the attractive U. S. Forest Service Headquarters to the left of the road. From time to time smaller stands of pine and spruce show where the Service has replanted forests which were burned or cut down in the early days. These seedlings come from their nursery near MONUMENT.

The road joins U. S. 24 at WOODLAND PARK, once a logging center and now a popular summer resort. Our By-Way tour continues east on U. S. 24 to a junction where you drop down into GREEN MOUNTAIN FALLS and CHIPITA. These lovely mountain resorts are like Swiss villages with their attractive year-round houses.

Once more the road joins U. S. 24 and goes through CASCADE, over UTE PASS, through MANITOU SPRINGS and back to COLORADO SPRINGS.

Pikes Peak as seen from Rampart Range ▶

Gold Camp Circle

By-Way Tour No. 4

The very name CRIPPLE CREEK conjures up visions of rich gold strikes and mining boom days. Some gold had been found in the vicinity in 1874 and 1884, but experienced mining men declared there was no gold here in quantity — the terrain wasn't right.

It took an inexperienced cowboy to light the fuse that made CRIPPLE CREEK one of the richest mining camps in history. Bob Womack prospected from time to time as he herded the cattle in Poverty Gulch. He found some "color" and took the ore to COLORADO CITY to be assayed. The report was so good he promptly got drunk and sold his claim, the El Paso, for $500. This same claim became the GOLD KING MINING CO., producing over $5,000,000 in gold. Bob Womack died a pauper.

CRIPPLE CREEK became known as the "Tenderfoot Camp" because it was through such inexperienced persons as Womack and others that some of the largest producing mines were discovered. Another man threw his hat into the air and dug a shaft where it landed. The resulting mine was a large producer.

Winfield Scott Stratton, who became a millionaire, was a carpenter turned prospector who found golden globules after his campfire died down one night. Thus came about the discovery of the INDEPENDENCE and WASHINGTON mines which he finally sold to an English syndicate for $11,000,000.

To reach CRIPPLE CREEK our By-Way tour leaves COLORADO SPRINGS via U. S. 24 through MANITOU SPRINGS, following FOUNTAIN CREEK. The early French trappers called it "Fontaine qui Bouille" meaning "fountain that boils." The stream actually looks as though it is boiling as it hurries down the steep hillsides.

You enter PIKE NATIONAL FOREST, one of the largest in the state. Along the highway, you will see beautiful stands of Englemann spruce, western yellow and lodgepole pine, and Douglas fir. Blue columbine flourishes in the aspen groves, and the pink and red fairy trumpets grow profusely on the sandy road cuts.

Dark granite cliffs close in on UTE PASS named for the Indians who claimed this area. They used the Pass coming from SOUTH PARK to bathe in the healing waters at MANITOU.

The pass has a dark and ugly history since it was the scene of many murders commited by the "Bloody Espinosas" brothers, who, in addition to other bandits, lay in wait in the neighboring rocky fissures and robbed people going and coming from the gold camps.

CASCADE was founded in 1886 and is best known as the entrance to the PIKES PEAK HIGHWAY. Now U. S. 24 climbs up above the creek and by-passes the lovely resort towns of CHIPITA and GREEN MOUNTAIN FALLS below. An alternate road leads through them.

The highway makes a wide swing northwestward around the north base of PIKES PEAK. At WOODLAND PARK, it turns southwest to DIVIDE. State 67 turns south here for CRIPPLE CREEK, 16 miles away.

However, our By-Way tour continues on U. S. 24 to FLORISSANT which was once a busy division point on the MIDLAND RAILROAD. You turn left on State 143 to the PETRIFIED FORESTS. Here a living forest of lodgepole pine and spruce grows amid petrified stumps of giant sequoias (California redwoods) and other subtropical trees.

COLORADO PETRIFIED FOREST (fee) has one large stump and a very interesting museum and lodge with fireplace made of petrified wood.

At PIKE PETRIFIED FOREST (fee) just beyond is another good museum. They have a well-marked footpath which winds among 15 stumps and logs which have been excavated. You'll see a living pine tree growing out of a petrified stump 15 feet across. The only petrified trio in the world rises majestically. On examination you'll find that this trio has a common root which means the original tree was 27 feet in diameter.

Many million years ago this area was an ancient lake bed. Giant cedars, sequoias and other trees lived on its bank. A great upheaval took place forcing up volcanoes which erupted and covered the trees and lake with lava or pumice.

Then petrification took place which accounts for the trees as they are today. You cannot take any petrified wood, but you are allowed to dig in a nearby hillside, where you'll find good specimen of early marine life, insects, leaves, ferns and shells imprinted on the pumice.

Our By-Way tour continues on State 143, a winding, well-graded road which twists and turns through lovely pine forests and wide hay meadows. Occasional ranches are seen. To the east, PIKES PEAK rears majestically, and glimpses of the snow-capped SANGRE DE CRISTO range may be seen to the south.

The road climbs to a high grassy rolling plateau, turns east rather abruptly and suddenly CRIPPLE CREEK appears, tucked into the steep west shoulder of mighty PIKES PEAK. The barren hills surrounding the town are pock-marked with yellow and grey mine dumps and prospect holes. It was named for a small creek which meanders through the area. MT. PISGAH, the sharp-coned mountain to the west, stands guard.

Actually CRIPPLE CREEK is located on the richest paying volcano in existence. Geologists now say that great masses of volcanic rock were spewed up in prehistoric times. Gold and telluride of gold clung to this molten lava and solidified, sometimes in whole chambers of almost free gold. It's like a tale from the Arabian Nights.

The district's fabulous history is preserved in the museum at the end of Bennett Avenue, which was formerly the Midland Terminal Railroad station.

The Portland Mine in Victor

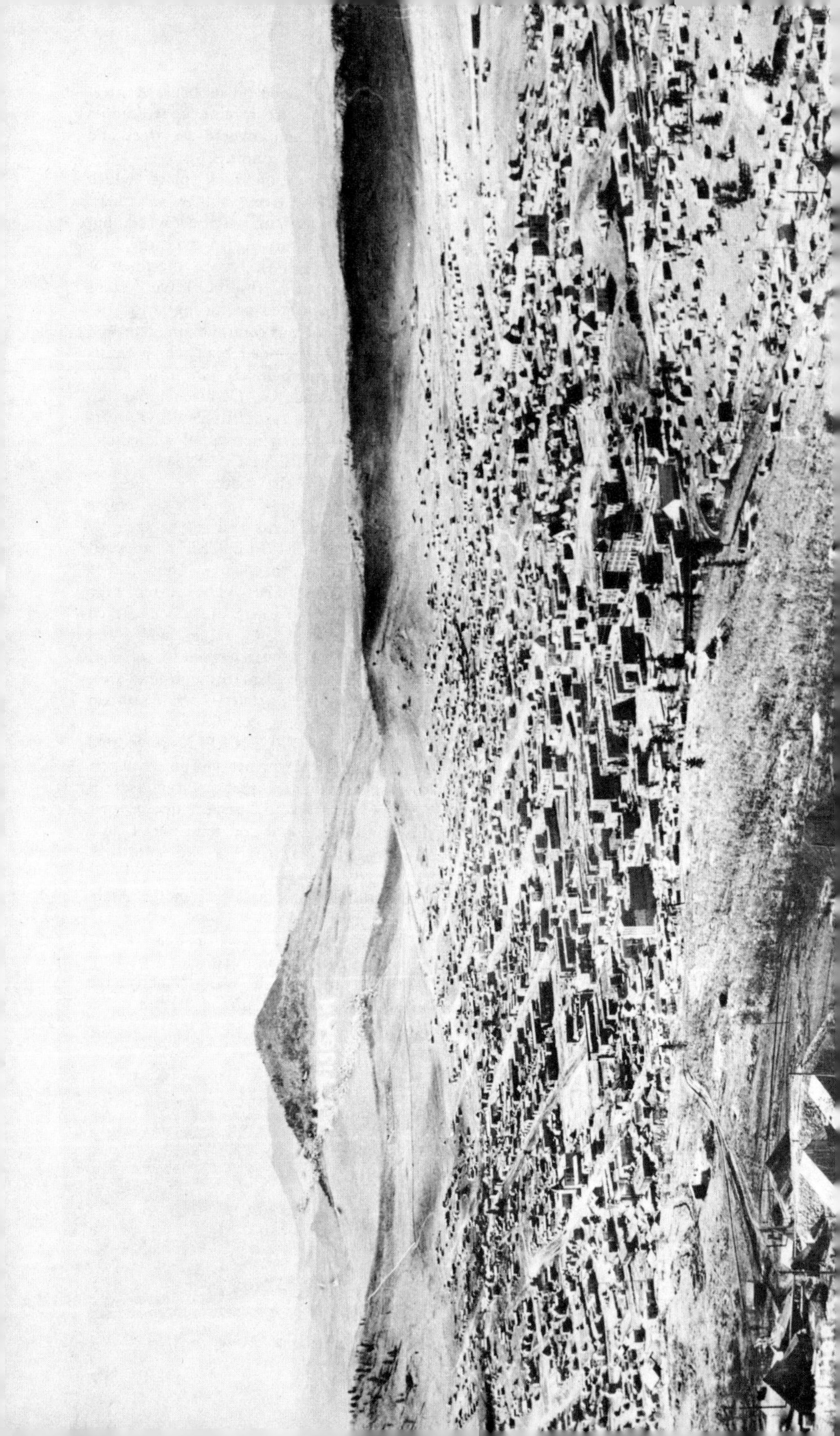

The Imperial Hotel has been renovated with room and meal accomodations and delightful gay 90's melodramas are produced in their theater during the summer.

The MOLLIE KATHLEEN MINE conducts a safe, clean tour through its working mine which has been producing gold and other ores since 1892. Their mineral display is superior.

Leaving CRIPPLE CREEK you continue south on State 67. The road cuts its way through the mountainside cluttered with hoists, shaft houses, railroad tracks and ore dumps for the entire six miles.

The hairpin curved highway passes a number of ghost towns — Anaconda, Elkton, Mound City, Arequa, lie in the gulches with only remnants of buildings, brick foundations and abandoned machinery or corrugated iron shacks to show where millions of dollars in gold have been dug and processed.

Log cribbing along the road keeps the mine dumps from burying the highway beneath tons of debris.

A swing around SQUAW MOUNTAIN and the road goes through a rocky cut. There before you is a dramatic panorama — VICTOR, hanging on the side of a steep hill, while above and below are tier upon tier of terraced dumps and shaft houses. It isn't unusual to see men digging for gold in their own back yards. And since uranium has been found here, it is being mined also.

A side trip north up the old narrow gauge railroad bed leads to GOLDFIELD, where the FLORENCE and CRIPPLE CREEK RAILROAD yards were located. ALTMAN on BULL MOUNTAIN is where there was so much fighting during CRIPPLE CREEK labor troubles.

Across the way on BATTLE MOUNTAIN is INDEPENDENCE, where Stratton made his millions. Then on through MIDWAY to CAMERON, where another railroad swung across a grassy meadow after its long hard climb from COLORADO SPRINGS.

In its hey-day the CRIPPLE CREEK district was served by three railroads — MIDLAND TERMINAL and CRIPPLE CREEK SHORT LINE (both from COLORADO SPRINGS) and the FLORENCE AND CRIPPLE CREEK from FLORENCE, COLORADO, 30 miles to the south. In addition there were two electric tramways — the highline and the lowline.

The district was torn several times by labor strife with violence erupting from time to time and people killed.

From VICTOR you have a choice of three ways to return to COLORADO SPRINGS. The simplest is to return from VICTOR to CRIPPLE CREEK and take State 67 north to DIVIDE on U. S. 24. Be sure to pause a moment just as the road tops the hill out of CRIPPLE CREEK. Glance back at a never-to-be-forgotten sight — a billion dollar cow pasture which confounded the experts.

The broad paved highway offers spectacular vistas of SOUTH PARK and the CONTINENTAL DIVIDE to the west. Remnants of the old roadbed of the MIDLAND TERMINAL may be seen from time to time.

A few miles north of CRIPPLE CREEK you'll see a ramshackle stone and brick building with a cross on the roof standing in the center of a plowed field and slowly tumbling down. A couple of other buildings and a rakish row of fire hydrants are all that remain of GILLETT, where the only bull fight in COLORADO was fought in 1895.

Another route from CRIPPLE CREEK is to take State 336 along one of the most scenic roads in COLORADO. Built as the CRIPPLE CREEK SHORT LINE from COLORADO SPRINGS, it was ridden by Theodore Roosevelt when he visited the state. He was so impressed by its scenery and engineering skill that he said any description would bankrupt the English language.

When the railroad was abandoned it became the CORLEY HIGHWAY, but is now called the GOLD CAMP ROAD. It is full of exciting thrills for it drops nearly 4,000 feet by a series of sweeping loops, curves and ledge grades which shoot through tunnels and out over high wooden trestles until it reaches COLORADO SPRINGS, about 30 miles beyond.

The third route is via State 67 through PHANTOM CANYON to State 220 and U. S. 50. This is another exciting mountain road following the old FLORENCE AND CRIPPLE CREEK right-of-way. Curves, switch-backs, deep canyons and spectacular scenery give the narrow, graded, winding road an off-the-beaten-path flavor.

Return to COLORADO SPRINGS via State 220 and 115, or to CANON CITY or PUEBLO via State 220 and U. S. 50.

◀ *Cripple Creek as it was in 1897*

Horn of Plenty

By-Way Tour No. 5

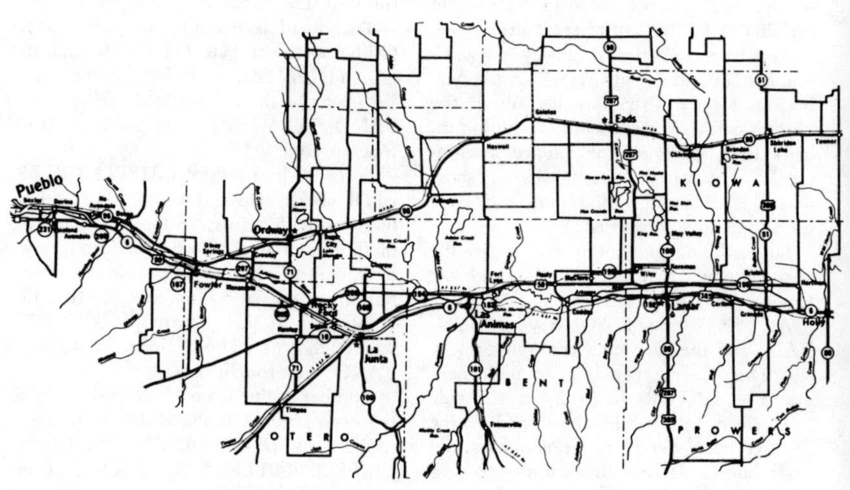

The most historic and best known river in COLORADO in the early days was the ARKANSAS RIVER which marked the dividing line between France's Louisiana to the north and Spain's Mexico to the south.

Earliest records say that Coronado followed the river upstream in 1541 until he saw the SPANISH PEAKS which helped him find his way back to Mexico after his unsuccessful search for Quivera, legendary city of gold.

Lt. Zebulon Pike and his party, who were sent to survey the newly purchased Louisiana Territory in 1806, reportedly got their first glimpse of the "great blue mountain" which was later to bear his name from along the high ground on this river near present day LAS ANIMAS.

Indians, explorers, trappers, traders and immigrants all stuck close to the river valley to insure water and grass for their stock. The SANTA FE TRAIL followed the river. After the middle of the 19th Century great cattle empires grew up and longhorn steers took over where once great herds of buffalo, antelope and deer roamed.

Until irrigation was introduced this region was considered a part of the "Great American Desert." Today the towns along the ARKANSAS VALLEY are like translucent green beads strung on the silver river. It is truly a horn of plenty land.

Our By-Way tour starts at PUEBLO following U. S. 50 east paralleling the south bank of the ARKANSAS RIVER. About 20 miles east where the HUERFANO RIVER empties into the ARKANSAS is the site of the famous AUTOBEES RANCH built by a French trader, Charles Autobees, in 1840, and for many years an important trading post.

FOWLER is a cattle shipping point. Beyond is MANZANOLA (apple orchard) where tons of apples, melons and vegetables are raised and shipped. The entire valley from here to LAMAR is lush with crops irrigated by water from the ARKANSAS and its tributaries.

ROCKY FORD is famous as the home of the Rocky Ford cantaloupe developed by George W. Swink in the '90's. If you're lucky enough to be here on Melon Day in September, they'll give you all the melons you can eat. In addition they raise carloads of watermelons, cucumbers, onions and sugar beets.

The most surprising crop to the visitor, though, are the acres of brilliant red, yellow and orange zinnias raised for seed. Free seeds are available for the asking. SWINK was named for the developer of the cantaloupe who also promoted the first irrigation in this area.

LA JUNTA (the junction) was founded in 1875 as a shipping point for wagon trains on the Santa Fe Trail. Today it is best known as the home of the KO-SHARE INDIANS, a Boy Scout Troup which devotes part of its time to keeping alive the dances, customs and costumes of the American Indian. A real treat is to see the KOSHARES dance.

Be sure to visit their beautiful KIVA MUSEUM at 18th street and Santa Fe Avenue, a replica of the southwestern Indian pueblo kivas or ceremonial rooms. In addition to this room, they have a fine Indian Art Museum and a little theater.

The FORT BENT MUSEUM in Court House Park has Indian artifacts, fossils, historic relics including a Concord Coach, and a scale model of BENT'S FORT which was located about ten miles east of town.

If you are interested in seeing giant dinosaur tracks in their natural habitat, take State 109 straight south to HIGBEE. A mile east on the banks of the PURGA-TOIRE RIVER 18 giant tracks of Tyrannosaurus Rex, one of the fiercest of ancient reptiles, appear in a straight path. Nearby are footprints of Triceratops, an ancestor of the rhinoceros.

Our By-Way tour crosses the ARKANSAS RIVER at LA JUNTA and turns northeast on State 194. Eight miles beyond is where BENT'S FORT was built in 1828 by William Bent and his three brothers. Designated as a NATIONAL HISTORIC SITE, the old fort is being restored by the NATIONAL PARK SERVICE.

BENT'S FORT was the biggest rendezvous in this area for Indians, trappers, plainsmen, Mexicans, traders, adventurers, and even Government troops. It was an oasis in the desert once the Santa Fe Trail became popular.

The FORT was more than a trading post — it was a large isolated community. The roster of well-known men who stopped or lived here from time to time includes Bill Williams, Dick Wootten, Kit Carson, John C. Fremont, and many, many others.

General Kearny stopped here with his army in 1848 enroute to Santa Fe at the beginning of the Mexican War. During the '49er gold rush to California the FORT grew in importance. It was abandoned in 1852 and there is a difference of opinion as to the real reason.

At any event, William Bent moved about forty miles east where he built a stone fort in 1853. Later he sold this fort to the Government and it was named FORT LYON. In 1866 the river began to cut away the bank nearby, so FORT LYON was moved 20 miles west to its present site.

State 194 leads to LAS ANIMAS, named for the nearby river, EL RIO DE LAS ANIMAS PERDIDOS EN PURGATORIO (The River of Lost Souls in Purgatory), which empties into the ARKANSAS here. Today the river is called the PURGATOIRE, but the cowboys call it "Picketwire."

Once LAS ANIMAS was a great cattle center and shipping point for buffalo

A replica of Bent's Fort

meat. Even today you'll see real cowboys wearing high-heeled boots and ten-gallon hats. But sheep have replaced some of the cattle ranches and others were broken up into irrigated farms.

BOGGSVILLE, two miles southeast on State 101, was the first permanent settlement here. The large adobe house built by Thomas O. Boggs in 1866 still stands. Kit Carson and his family lived at BOGGSVILLE for some time before he died, but his house was destroyed by flood. Mr. and Mrs. Boggs took the seven Carson children into their home and reared them after Kit and his wife died just a few months apart.

Nearby is JOHN MARTIN RESERVOIR, first called CADDOA, after the Indian tribe which once lived here. In the fall there is excellent hunting for ducks and geese.

Continuing south on State 101 to RULE CREEK you will see interesting Indian Petroglyphs on the cliffs. Some authorities claim they date back 5,000 years and are duplicates of many found in several other parts of the world.

Our By-Way tour continues east from LAS ANIMAS five miles to FORT LYON which has been converted into a Veterans' Administration Hospital. KIT CARSON MUSEUM is on the reservation. The famous scout and his wife both died here in 1868. Their bodies were moved later to Taos, New Mexico.

Next on State 50 is HASTY. Four miles south is JOHN MARTIN DAM and below it is HASTY LAKE, well-equipped for swimming, boating, picnicking, camping and here the fisherman will find plenty of bullheads, wall-eyed pike, black bass, trout and channel catfish.

Just before reaching LAMAR, on the bluffs to the right above the ARKANSAS RIVER is the site of the stone fort which Bent built in 1853. At LAMAR opposite the railroad station you will see the well-known statue, MADONNA OF THE TRAIL, which honors the women pioneers.

For those interested in Indian artifacts follow State 192 west about eight miles to the site of a Cheyenne Indian village. Beads, stone axes and arrowheads are found here.

Rockhounds will want to visit the PETRIFIED FOREST. You drive two miles south of LAMAR on U. S. 287, take a country road east for about one mile, then angle southeast. Here on the prairies and along the arroyo banks you will find agate, petrified wood, fossils and oyster shells from an ancient sea.

East of LAMAR on U. S. 50 is GRANADA, site of the camp where many Japanese families were interned during World War II, and beyond is HOLLY, almost on the Kansas state line.

Our By-Way tour retraces U. S. 50 west from LAMAR for eight miles, then turns north on U. S. 287 to EADS, trade center for a large dry farming area.

A side trip east on State 96 to CHIVINGTON, then north about ten miles takes you to the site of the SAND CREEK BATTLE GROUND. This is perhaps the most controversial of all historical battles fought in the state of COLORADO. Reams have been written for and against Colonel John Chivington, who led the Third Regiment against an encampment of Indians and almost completely annihilated them. Probably no one will ever know the true facts.

Our By-Way tour turns west from EADS on State 96 across rolling brown hills which in spring and early summer are carpeted with beautiful western prairie flowers. First come the white, pink, and yellow primroses followed by the red, blue, yellow and white locos. The cacti take over in late May with silky blood-red, purple, yellow and white blossoms. Creamy white yucca candles point skyward.

Then come the blue penstemons, orange cowboy's delight, and dock shaded from green through brown. Later in the summer yellow predominates in the sunflowers, paper flowers, rabbit brush and sundrops. In addition, you'll see blazing stars, blue larkspur, purple verbena and white evening stars.

Approaching ORDWAY cultivated fields appear again due to irrigation. Nearby LAKES MEREDITH and HENRY offer good fishing, boating and hunting.

CROWLEY has a real "wild west" history. In the 1880's wild horses were trapped near here, "broken," then shipped to England for army use.

Now State 96 meets the ARKANSAS RIVER, turns northwest and parallels both the river and U. S. 50 on the south bank the rest of the way through NEPESTA, BOONE and NORTH AVONDALE into PUEBLO.

Koshare Indians doing the Ghost Dance ▶

Spanish Peaks' Country

By-Way Tour No. 6

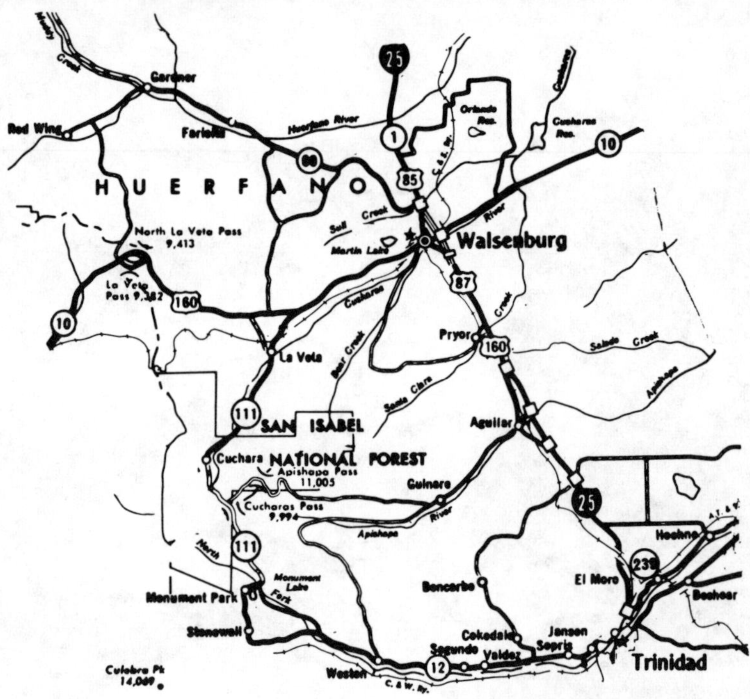

The Ute Indians once claimed this region, then came the Spanish conquistadores, followed by the mountain men and fur trappers, the traders, the gold seekers, and finally the permanent settlers. Our By-Way tour follows their trails through thriving towns, Spanish-American hamlets, coal fields and picturesque country which beckons the vacationist.

The SPANISH PEAKS dominate the country and their very name sets the keynote of the area where there are as many, if not more, names of Spanish than of English origin. Economically and politically the region is part of COLORADO, but culturally it is closer to neighboring New Mexico because so many of the inhabitants are descendants of the early Spanish settlers.

Our By-Way tour starts at WALSENBURG, seat of HUERFANO COUNTY, which was originally called LA PLAZA DE LOS LEONES (Square of the Lions) by the original Spanish landowners. The development of nearby coal mines and the building of the railroad boomed the town. Today agriculture, cattle and sheep raising add their share to its prosperity.

You take State 69 northwest out of WALSENBURG following the old Spanish Trail that ran from Taos and Santa Fe, New Mexico, to Ft. Laramie, Wyoming. To the left are vast coal fields, and the road crosses rough hilly country just south of the WET MOUNTAINS.

At BADITO you enter the HUERFANO (Orphan) VALLEY, which takes its name from the volcanic butte which stands alone east of Interstate 70 north of WALSENBURG. Fossil bones of the three-toed horse have been found in nearby canyons.

Old FORT TALPA, an adobe outpost built by the Spaniards in 1820, still stands in FARISITA. The lonely little church across the river is called a morada and belongs to the Penitente Brothers. These dedicated men still celebrate Passion Week according to ancient rites. Visitors are NOT welcome.

Multi-colored GARDNER CONE to the left was once a landmark. Pinon pines cover the hillsides and their tasty nuts or seeds are eagerly gathered by the Spanish-American residents to eat and to sell.

GARDNER is in the midst of comparatively unspoiled and uncommercial country. The village is chiefly an outfiting point for pack trips and camping. Spanish holidays are still celebrated here as they were a hundred years ago.

State 69 follows BIG MUDDY CREEK through wild and broken country to PROMONTORY DIVIDE, then drops down into the WET MOUNTAIN VALLEY to WESTCLIFFE.

Our By-Way tour turns left at GARDNER on State 150 to MALACHITE where Tom Sharp built a trading post in 1870.

The dirt road continues through RED WING and HUERFANO PARK which is excellent for big game. Eventually the road climbs over MOSCA PASS to the SAND DUNES in the SAN LUIS VALLEY (via jeep or horseback only).

You turn south from MALACHITE on State 150, a one-lane dirt road with occasional turnouts wandering along for 13 miles to NORTH LA VETA PASS (U. S. 160). This pass is located between the SANGRE DE CRISTOS and CULEBRA (Snake) RANGES. As you begin to descend you can see, to the right, the old LA VETA PASS road which was built with many switchbacks on the old narrow gauge railroad bed. The famous "muleshoe" curve is still there.

Autumn turns LA VETA PASS into a flaming spectacle. Stunning blends of red, orange and yellow aspen and scrub oak paint the mountainside during the fall. At the junction of State 111 you turn south to LA VETA (vein), a Spanish hamlet.

The road continues south into SAN ISABEL NATIONAL FOREST through scrub oak and pinon pine to CUCHARAS CAMPS. To the left you'll see the DEVIL'S STAIR STEP, one of the huge rock walls which radiate like spokes of a wheel from the SPANISH PEAKS to the east.

The highway starts climbing now through Ponderosa and yellow pine forests. To the right a side road takes you to BEAR and BLUE LAKES set amid striking red stone walls carved in fantastic shapes. Wild deer frequently cross your path, so if you are as adept with a gun as with a fishing reel, you may want to return for fine deer, bear and wild turkey hunting.

State 111 tops CUCHARAS PASS. A side trip for the adventurous turns east from here along State 232 past the two SPANISH PEAKS. Here may be found ancient altars to sun gods, Indian petroglyphs and pictographs, and other evidence that the Indians revered these mountains.

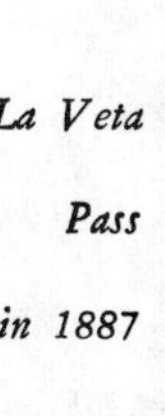

La Veta

Pass

in 1887

Our By-Way tour continues on State 111 past MONUMENT LAKE to STONEWALL, named for the strange stone dikes which occur at intervals along the ROCKIES from Canada to Mexico. There are lovely panoramic views of twin-coned CULEBRA PEAK, a landmark to the south, and sandstone-capped RED PEAK.

Trails and dirt roads lead the adventurous to WHISKEY CREEK PASS on the west and to TERCIO and VERNEJO PARK across the border south into New Mexico.

Historic STONEWALL was the site of armed battles among homesteaders, land grant owners and cattlemen last century. Bitter fueds developed.

At STONEWALL our By-Way tour turns east on State 12 following the PUGATOIRE RIVER. At one time several interesting Spanish-American hamlets with their musical names such as CORDOVA PLAZA, MEDINAS PLAZA, VELESQUEZ, ZARCILLO PLAZA, and SAN JUAN PLAZA were strung along the river. In the early days under Spanish rule these were farming communities. Later they became dependent for their livelihood on the coal mines which seam the neighboring hillsides.

Most of the villages have been moved or destroyed because of the building of TRINIDAD DAM and RESERVOIR. At one time each small hamlet was almost a one family settlement. The older villages were built around a plaza or square typical of the Spanish custom. What old adobe churches remain are picturesque.

No matter how poor, each Spanish-American adobe house has its own nicho (niche) with a santo (saint). Some are old family statues carved during the height of the santo period. Before them burn wax candles.

Be sure to pause at one of the Spanish cemeteries. Usually dry and barren, the hand-carved wooden crosses are hung with bright pink, red and yellow wax or paper flowers and decorated with colorful rocks and pebbles.

At the junction of Interstate 25 and U. S. 85 is TRINIDAD (Trinity) whose chief industry was coal mining. In addition to the large Spanish-American population there are many persons of Italian descent whose fathers came in the early days to work in the coal mines.

TRINIDAD'S crooked streets give it a foreign flavor. The town has seen much history from the time it was an Indian ceremonial ground through the coming of the Spaniards, the French trappers, and finally, the Americans following the Military Branch of the SANTA FE TRAIL.

TRINIDAD became very important when "Uncle" Dick Wootten established his toll road in 1865 over RATON PASS about 12 miles south on the COLORADO-NEW MEXICO state line (Interstate 25).

Two interesting pioneer homes have been restored by the Colorado State Historical Society. The BLOOM MANSION is a gem of Victorian architecture. Rancher Don Felipe Baca's two-story adobe home shows how the early-day Spanish-American landowners lived.

There are interesting side trips out of TRINIDAD. For the collector of Indian artifacts, U. S. 160 which zigzags east to the Kansas line is good hunting territory. This was part of the "dust bowl" of the '30's which uncovered ancient Indian waterholes, which made hunting easier.

FISHER PEAK to the south of town has at least eight lava flows with interesting rock formations. BARELA (State 160) was once the home of Senator Barela who lived like a feudal lord at his nearby ranch, RIVERA. Trails leading to RATON MESA reward the traveler with fields of wild flowers, a variety of wild game, and Indian relics.

BRANSON is the gateway to TOLLGATE CANYON through which Texas longhorns were driven on the GOODNIGHT TRAIL. Sixteen miles south is MESA DE MAYA (May Flower Table-

Bloom Mansion in Trinidad

56

land) where there are Indian petroglyphs chiseled on the cliffs. Folsom man points, stone hoes and scrapers, as well as bones from bison extinct for 20,000 years have been found here.

Spanish horsemen in shining armor, together with foot soldiers and Indian slaves, are believed to have come across this area with Coronado in the 15th century searching for QUIVERA, legendary city of gold.

Old water holes and buffalo wallows near KIM, PRITCHETT and SPRINGFIELD have also yielded Indian relics.

From SPRINGFIELD you may return north on U. S. 160 and 287 to LAMAR, or go back to PRITCHETT and take State 101 to LAS ANIMAS on U. S. 50. Then turn west to LA JUNTA where you angle southwest on U. S. 350 to TRINIDAD or State 10 to WALSENBURG.

If you choose U. S. 350 from LA JUNTA you'll follow the old Military Branch of the SANTA FE TRAIL which once boomed with covered wagon traffic, and ran from BENT'S FORT, near LA JUNTA, to Taos and Santa Fe, New Mexico.

This trail is through wild, desolate arid country, with only desert plants such as yucca, cacti, mesquite and sagebrush able to survive. The red and yellow blossoms of the cane cactus are particularly beautiful here in June.

A few pin-point villages break the otherwise long solid stretches. Near TINPAS is HOLE-IN-THE-ROCK which was once a watering place on the trail. THATCHER is one of the few places in the world where helium gas is found, but the government has capped the wells. In the distance to the west the SPANISH PEAKS stand starkly above the plains.

A half-mile west of TYRONE is HOLE-IN-THE-PRAIRIE, another watering spot for the SANTA FE and the CHISHOLM TRAILS bringing longhorns from Texas. Indians used this for a rendezvous, too, and many battles were fought over its possession. Look for arrowheads.

Five miles beyond and to the left is the road leading to PURGATOIRE CANYON, grotesquely eroded. Prehistoric Indians carved petroglyphs here, too, and it's a happy hunting ground for the collector of petrified fossils.

Large prairie dog towns may be seen from the highway, where the frisky little animals sit up on their hind feet and stare back at you unless you frighten them. Then, with a flick of their tails, they disappear into their holes. The tiny "Billy" owl moves into their abandoned homes.

Near EARL is a green oasis called Sunflower Valley where good crops are raised thanks to irrigation. HOEHNE, off the highway four miles, is noted because here, the first irrigation ditch was built in the area using water from the PURGATOIRE RIVER.

Our By-Way tour returns to TRINIDAD, then picks up northbound Interstate 25. To the west of the highway winding country roads lead to coal mining hamlets.

Just off Interstate 25 is LUDLOW, which has an infamous history. A coal strike in 1913-14 brought disaster to the town. The miners and their sympathizers set up a tent city, and the governor of COLORADO sent the State Militia to keep order. Somehow, fighting broke out and several miners were killed. The tent city was set afire and several women and children died as a result. It was a tragic affair. The strike was lost, but the "Ludlow Massacre" brought about better working conditions in mines throughout the country.

AGUILAR is another Spanish-American community. Our By-Way tour ends at WALSENBURG under the shadow of the SPANISH PEAKS.

Wives of Ludlow strikers protesting against "Mother Jones" imprisonment at Trinidad

Canon City and Gold Belt Circle

By-Way Tour No. 7

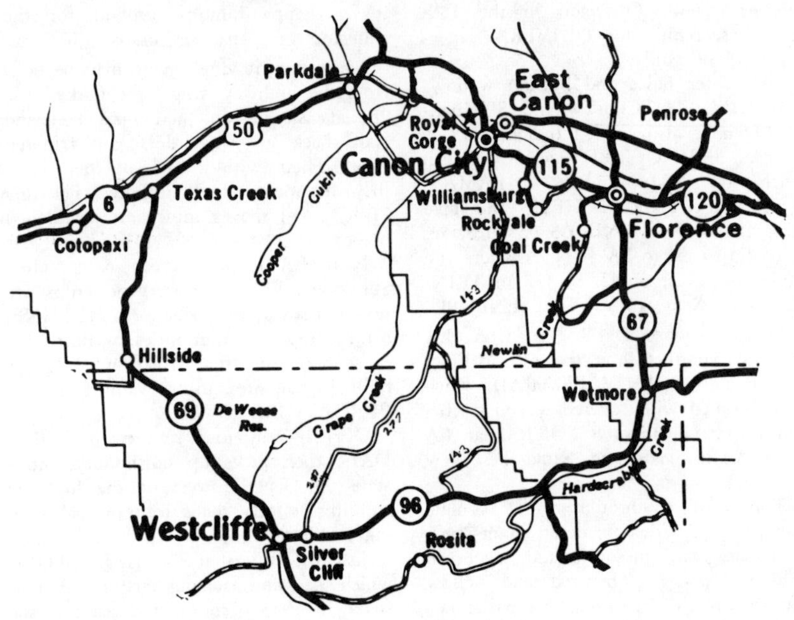

If you enjoy spectacular scenery, back country roads, collecting ore and rock specimen, exploring caves, taking pictures, riding horseback, hiking, or just plain loafing — this By-Way tour is for you. It's the kind of country where you can spend a satisfying day or week or month and still come back for more.

The tour itself starts in CANON CITY, but can easily be taken from PUEBLO, COLORADO SPRINGS, or DENVER by adding an additional 40 minutes, one hour, or two-and-one-half hours of driving time.

CANON CITY is a lovely small town nestled at the eastern edge of the spectacular GRAND CANYON (ROYAL GORGE) OF THE ARKANSAS RIVER in the fertile ARKANSAS VALLEY. The region is particularly favored by a delightful climate with no great temperature extremes such as many parts of the country experience.

A stone marker in STATE PARK near the PENITENTIARY shows the approximate site where Lt. Zebulon Pike and his party camped in 1806. Here he celebrated his 28th birthday and from here he explored the ROYAL GORGE, thinking he was enroute to the headwaters of the Red River. Also from here he and his party left to cross "the great white mountain" (SANGRE DE CRISTO RANGE) into the SAN LUIS VALLEY where they were captured by the Spaniards and taken to prison in Santa Fe.

Indian hunters, mountain men and fur trappers knew this area, but the first white settlement was made in 1858 when gold seekers came through enroute to the gold fields in SOUTH PARK and GREGORY GULCH.

You'll want to visit the ANSON RUDD LOG CABIN, one of the first houses, east of the MUNICIPAL BUILDING at 6th and River Streets. The MU-

SEUM in the MUNICIPAL BUILDING houses a wonderful collection of 16 blue flint axes found along nearby Grape Creek, other Indian artifacts, historic relics and a fine exhibit of archeological and wildlife specimen.

The forbidding stone walls and buildings of the STATE PENITENTIARY (visitors permitted) at the western edge of town are backed up against a picturesque "hogback" mountain which not even the most daring of convicts would attempt to climb to escape.

An interesting By-Way tour leads north on State 143. Six miles out there are Indian pictographs on the west side of the road. A mile north is the GARDEN PARK DINOSAUR MONUMENT showing the site where five giant dinosaurs were excavated and shipped to museums. This area is a happy hunting ground for the rock and fossil collector because both agate and jasperized dinosaur bones are found.

Hiking along Felch Creek a couple of miles beyond you may pick up red agate, red jasper, geodes, alabaster and more fossil bones. Another two miles is RED CANONS PARK, a scenic area, where gigantic red sandstone monoliths dominate the small arroyos or canyons. It's a favorite picnic spot.

The exciting SKYLINE DRIVE is taken by going west from CANON CITY on U. S. 50 for three and one-half miles to a marker. Turn right and climb quickly on a one-way well-graded road which circles the crest of the huge "hogback" mountain behind the penitentiary. You'll get a panoramic view of the mouth of the ROYAL GORGE and the ARKANSAS RIVER to the right. Stretching north and south are the ROCKIES. To the left CANON CITY and the beautiful countryside are spread below like a huge crazy quilt. This is a breathtaking view in May during the BLOSSOM FESTIVAL when the whole area is a sea of pink and white apple blossoms.

To the south of CANON CITY is WET MOUNTAIN VALLEY with its picturesque ghost towns and majestic scenery nestling between stalwart forests with their aromatic mountain air. That's the target for our By-Way tour which turns south from CANON CITY on State 143.

For the rockhound a quick side trip to the left at the first fork in the road takes you to SPECIMEN RIDGE or CURIO HILL, a low limestone ridge running in a northwest direction. Beautiful banded agate is found here.

State 143 enters SAN ISABEL NATIONAL FOREST and pictorial OAK CREEK CANYON with its spruce, fir and pine forests. (State 277 leads directly to SILVER CLIFF.) Continue on State 143 along OAK CREEK to ISLE, an old mining camp of the '80's. Very little remains of the old town which is now a summer resort. Mine dumps pock-mark the hillsides. The big producer, THE TERRIBLE, gave up enormous deposits of crystallized lead.

At the junction of State 96 turn west over barren, rough country to the BASSICK MINE which was once one of the richest gold and silver mines in the state. You can prospect the mine dumps for ore specimen. But don't go into abandoned mine tunnels — they are dangerous.

QUERIDA boomed with the BASSICK MINE. A few houses, shacks and brick foundations remain to remind you that this was once a prosperous mining camp.

A country road leads south to ROSITA built in 1876, another ghost town, named for the wild roses which grow so profusely. A few tumbled-down shacks tilt rakishly and foundations gape. The hillsides are gophered with mine holes and dumps.

Back to QUERIDA you continue on State 96 to SILVER CLIFF which in 1880 was the third largest city in COLORADO. It crept toward ghosthood long ago and has now settled to a tattered, comfortable old age. A remnant of the original town remains with some buildings leaning crazily. Each winter's snow takes its toll.

The iron-stained face of the cliff which faces the city produced almost pure horn silver (tinfoil-like layers) which set off the rush. After the surface silver was gathered, mine shafts were sunk with resulting rich silver pockets. The BULL-DOMINGO and the RACINE BOY were the two leading mines.

The GEYSER MINE, the biggest payer, was sunk into the crater of an extinct volcano which produced huge boulders coated with rich silver ore. After the boom broke, many homes were moved "in toto" from SILVER CLIFF to WEST-CLIFFE.

SILVER CLIFF as well as other silver mining camps folded during the panic of 1893 when silver was demonetized. Between SILVER CLIFF and WEST-CLIFFE, a mile away, is the old ramshackle CUSTER COUNTY COURT HOUSE, which belonged to SILVER CLIFF when it was county seat.

WESTCLIFFE, now the largest town in the WET MOUNTAIN VALLEY and the county seat, is not living on reminiscences. Bright geraniums fill the windows, lawns are neatly mowed, buildings are painted, and the store has plenty of supplies for ranchers and fly fishermen.

Ironically WESTCLIFFE came into being because of SILVER CLIFF. The DENVER & RIO GRANDE RAILROAD built a spur from CANON CITY to haul the ore from SILVER CLIFF and other mining camps.

The HOPE LUTHERAN CHURCH in WESTCLIFFE was built by the German colonists who came to the WET MOUNTAIN VALLEY in 1870. The original colony was a failure and many of the settlers left discouraged after crop failures. Some stayed, however, and the descendants of those pioneers still own many of the prosperous ranches which cover the valley.

Several country roads fan out of WESTCLIFFE through the valley south to delightful recreation spots. On the SANGRE DE CRISTOS the glaciers have receded leaving only their tracks — the cirques that cradle 52 small vivid lakes reflecting the blue sky and well-stocked with trout.

Deer and small animals abound. You can picnic, camp ride horseback or take pack trips into the mountains. Dude ranches are numerous. When you climb high turn your eyes from glacial altitudes and look down on dense forests, lush ranch country, and the high plains barely visible over the crests of the WET MOUNTAINS to the east.

The adventurous souls and the rockhounds should follow State 69 south paralleling the mountains to Beck's School. West from here at the base of the precipitous CRESTONE NEEDLES is MARBLE MOUNTAIN. A four-mile foottrail leads up MARBLE MOUNTAIN to MARBLE CAVE.

According to legends the early Spaniards called this "La Caverna del Oro" (the Cave of Gold), and they are supposed to have worked it successfully from the other side of the range. No one

Royal Gorge

knows who painted the large Maltese Cross near the entrance, but it has been there for more than a century. Actually, the cave is a volcanic fissure. It was partially explored in 1920 by a forest ranger who heard about it from an old Spanish woman who was then over one hundred years old.

Prehistoric plant and animal fossils are embedded in the canyon and cave walls. Attractive rock specimen can be found. There are seven additional caves, among them WOODMAN CAVE and BRIDAL CAVE. Guides and proper equipment are recommended for extensive exploration of any of these caves as they can be dangerous.

MOSCO PASS, a few miles south (accessible by foot, horseback or jeep), is where Lt. Pike and his party almost froze to death when they crossed the SANGRE DE CRISTOS into the SAN LUIS VALLEY to the west. State 69 continues south through GARDNER to WALSENBURG and TRINIDAD.

Our By-Way tour returns north to WESTCLIFFE, then swings northwest on State 69 up and down hills spotted with cedar and pinon pine to HILLSIDE. Roads leading west from this resort town take you to lovely picnic and camping spots, and to mountain lakes filled with fish.

An alternate route from HILLSIDE is via State 272 to COTOPAXI on U. S. 50. Across the ARKANSAS RIVER on the old mine dumps you can find malachite, pyrite, reddish garnet, and green gahnite crystals.

Another picturesque road takes off from State 69 and angles northeast down COPPER GULCH to either U. S. 50 or State 9 which takes you to the south side of the ROYAL GORGE BRIDGE or back on the south side of the ARKANSAS RIVER to CANON CITY.

Our By-Way tour stays on State 69 down Texas Creek to TEXAS CREEK on U. S. 50. Across the ARKANSAS RIVER and six miles north is DEVIL'S HOLE MINE where gem aquamarine and rose quartz are found in the feldspar and mica dumps.

Back to U. S. 50 you follow the churning ARKANSAS RIVER, then crossing it at PARKDALE swing northeast until the road tops a long curve. You turn right on State 9, winding around long switchbacks until you reach the top of the sagebrush studded mesa of the ROYAL GORGE. Here the highest auto bridge in the world (fee) spans the mighty GRAND CANYON of the ARKANSAS.

As you drive across the bridge you are suddenly transported into a breathtaking experience. Over a thousand feet below the silvery ribbon of the ARKANSAS RIVER twists and turns between gigantic red walls.

Inspiration Point to the south side of the bridge lures shutterbugs for unusual shots. You may follow a well-graded road, cross GRAPE CREEK, pass several picnic spots and return to CANON CITY from here. Back across the bridge you may ride the world's steepest incline railway (fee) down into the gorge, where you can gaze upward at almost perpendicular red granite walls. At the bottom you'll also see the unique hanging bridge, which is the only way the railroad can get through this narrow passage.

The ROYAL GORGE was a formidable obstacle to the railroad pushing its tracks westward to LEADVILLE. Tales as exciting as any TV Western tell the story of the pitched battle between the DENVER & RIO GRANDE and the SANTA FE RAILROADS for possession of this almost impassable gorge.

Equally exciting is the story of how men had to be suspended from the top by ropes to blast a shelf along the river for the railroad bed because the canyon was too narrow. The DENVER & RIO GRANDE won the fight through court proceedings and today their streamliners hug the canyon walls, making them echo with the diesel engines' hoarse horn.

About half way back to U. S. 50 to the right you'll see where a mountain has been quarried away. Most of this rock is feldspar used in making of glass and porcelain. Fine rock crystals, black tourmaline, beryl, red garnet and blue apatite are found here (permission required).

U. S. 50 makes a wide south curve passing the "hogback" with SKYLINE DRIVE. One final side trip off the highway to the right will take you to the mouth of the ROYAL GORGE through a number of tunnels carved through the solid red granite of FREMONT'S PEAK.

Back to U. S. 50 the highway swings around the "hogback" and into CANON CITY.

PART 3

TABLE OF CONTENTS

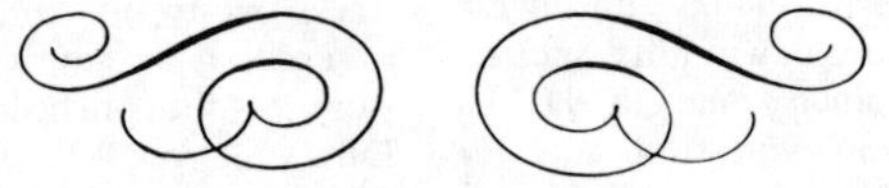

COLORADO

"Colorful COLORADO" — "The Silver State" — "The Centennial State" — "The Vacationer's State" — call it what you will, COLORADO, like its area, has something big to offer anyone who comes to visit — or to stay.

For the vacationist this is four-season country with each season presenting its own particular brand of fun. But all seasons share one thing — plenty of bright sunshine and clear blue skies. There are high mountains to climb; streams, lakes and rivers to fish, swim in and boat on; horseback, jeep, hiking and nature lovers' trails; innumerable picnic spots. Unexcelled skiing areas are noted for their powder snow. Ghost towns, resort towns, ranches, cities — take your pick. It's a rockhound's and shutterbug's paradise.

Historically, COLORADO is young-old since it wasn't actually settled to any extent until 1859. But the Indians knew this country well. Their ancestors lived here long before Columbus pleaded with Queen Isabella for her jewels to finance his ocean-going voyages as evidenced by Indian artifacts found in many places and the cliff dwellings at MESA VERDE.

Recorded history began almost 300 years ago when EL RIO DEL NORTE (The Great River of the North — shortened today to the RIO GRANDE) lured the Spanish Conquistadores in shining armor up its banks into the fertile SAN LUIS VALLEY. This influence is still felt throughout the region. Actually, COLORADO's southern state line is a parallel of latitude, but inside this straight boundary is a wavy one that marks the edge of the Spanish-speaking penetration. The southwestern part of the state, particularly the SAN LUIS VALLEY, is economically and politically a part of COLORADO, but culturally it belongs to New Mexico.

At one time much of this area came under the Mexican Land Grants when this region was ceded to the United States after the Mexican War resulting in many title disputes.

Lt. Zebulon Pike, by the Grace of God and his faithful party, was the first American to see part of this southwestern section. Mountain men, including famous Kit Carson, knew it well. Gold seekers sped across it enroute to the gold fields. But it wasn't until the ranchers and farmers came that the valleys blossomed into great green gardens.

Gunnison Country

By-Way Tour No. 1

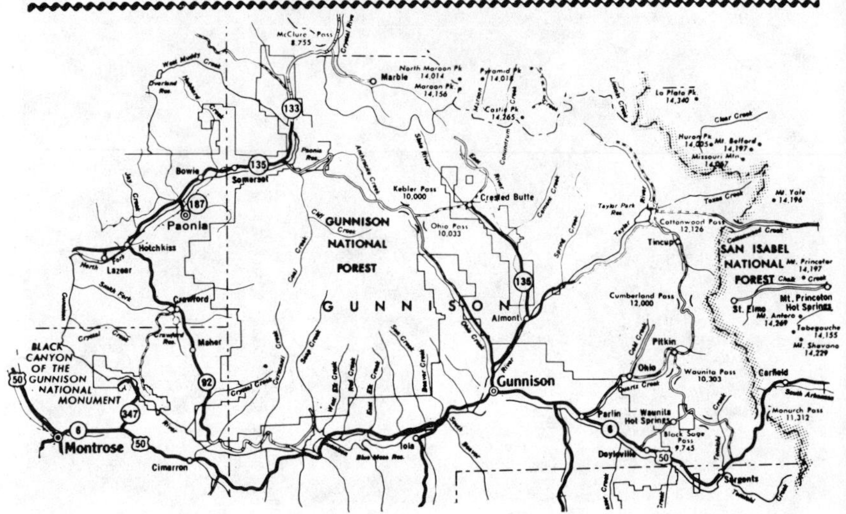

High mountain peaks, turbulent white-foamed rivers, gold and silver strikes, ghost towns and railroad builders' dreams dominate this By-Way tour of COLORADO.

Today the GUNNISON country, home of fighting trout, is synonymous with top-notch fishing and superb ranch country. The GUNNISON RIVER cuts a path from the mountains, drops down to sage-covered hills, gouges out the state's deepest gorge — the BLACK CANYON — and then meanders through former desert country to join the mighty COLORADO RIVER.

There was a day when this whole region rang with the miner's pick and shovel, the stamp mill's roar, and the sound of the narrow gauge railroad huffing and puffing over innumerable switchbacks to scale mountains and bring out pay dirt.

The area has seen the usual mining booms come and go with gold, silver, lead, copper, coal and other minerals having the spotlight directed on them. And always there is the chance that another mineral will be discovered in quantity or the price of ore will go up so the old mines may be reworked.

Even names exert much fascination — TINCUP, GOTHIC, PIE PLANT, CRESTED BUTTE, PITKIN — to name a few.

But the people who make the GUNNISON country prosper today are sturdy souls running great cattle and sheep ranches or turning their hands to cultivate the tourist. The GUNNISON region is unsurpassed as a vacationist's fondest dream. There are swimming, hiking, horseback riding, pack and jeep trips, rockhounding, botany trails for the flower lover, photography, camping and, of course, fishing. In fact, the GUNNISON area proudly makes its claim that it is second to none as a trout fishing paradise.

Our By-Way trip starts at SALIDA known as the "Heart of the Rockies," and easily accessible by excellent mountain highways from every corner of the state. You take U. S. 50 west and very soon the ARKANSAS VALLEY is left behind.

The road climbs up into GUNNISON NATIONAL FOREST through splendid forests of Ponderosa pine, spruce and fir to MONARCH PASS, at the top of the CONTINENTAL DIVIDE (11,386 feet). Long vistas are seen in every direction.

Our By-Way tour follows U. S. 50 around broad hairpin curves which take you down quickly to heavily-wooded TOMICHI (hot water) CREEK VALLEY. At SARGENTS the "helper" engines of the narrow gauge once waited to push the tiny trains back over MARSHALL PASS to SALIDA. From time to time you can see the abandoned railroad grade.

Just beyond is DOYLEVILLE. Turn right on another route to WAUNITA HOT SPRINGS, a favorite spa since Indian days. First a popular resort in 1885, it was revived in 1916. The sulphur and soda swimming pool still attracts visitors. A road leading north connects with PITKIN.

Our By-Way tour returns to U. S. 50 and continues to PARLIN where the PITKIN branch of the D&RG narrow gauge turned northeast. This was known as the CUMBERLAND PASS ROUTE. You take the right hand graveled road which leads to good fishing and hunting country, ghost towns and a rockhound's paradise.

The rockhound will want to turn right on a dirt road about four miles out of PARLIN. Less than a mile beyond is the old OPPORTUNITY MINE where specimen of blue beryl, creamy topaz, pink lepidolite and black tourmaline may be found in the dumps.

Go back to the main road, proceed another two miles and take another dirt road to the right. Above on the mountainside you can see the BROWN DERBY MINE, a famous pegmatite deposit, about two miles away (get permission to visit). Real bonanza was once found here by collectors in the form of watermelon tourmaline — green, white and red crystals. The dumps still yield pink tourmaline, bluish-green beryl, white topaz and lavender lepidolite.

Back on the main road, it is only about a mile to OHIO CITY, now a semi-ghost town with supplies for ranchers and vacationists. Founded in 1880 during the silver boom, it enjoyed a revival in the '90's when gold was discovered on GOLD CREEK running north from here.

The GOLD CREEK road leads to CARTER MINES, RAYMOND MINE, OLD LINKS MINE — all good hunting grounds for specimen. GOLD CREEK CAMP GROUND is a good place to pitch your tent, and there's trout fishing in the creek.

From OHIO CITY it's seven miles to PITKIN, founded in 1878, and named for a COLORADO governor. Wire silver assaying 80% solid silver brought miners by the thousands. The SILVER AGE, the SILENT FRIEND, the IRON CAP, and the RED JACKET were all good producers.

PITKIN seems to be dozing, waiting for another mine boom.

In the Black Canyon's deepest part, the depth ranges up to 2,425 feet

The Gunnison River winds its way through the deep-walled Black Canyon

From PITKIN you follow NORTH QUARTZ CREEK up the winding road over CUMBERLAND PASS. You'll see the site of QUARTZ marked now only with empty foundations. There are lovely views from the pass with weathered shaft houses and prospect holes showing where miners gophered for pay dirt. A shelf road snakes down into TINCUP.

This colorful mining camp was built on a broad alpine meadow. A radio program over one of DENVER'S radio stations has helped popularize it. According to one story, TINCUP was named because a miner brought a sample of gold-bearing sands to the assayer in a tin cup.

During TINCUP'S hey-day the JIMMY MACK and GOLD CUP MINES produced more than $2,000,000 in gold and silver. The ore was packed out on muleback through TINCUP PASS east over the CONTINENTAL DIVIDE to ST. ELMO in the ARKANSAS VALLEY, then shipped to smelters. TINCUP had a wild and wooly reputation with its full share of rough and dangerous characters.

The road goes north out of TINCUP past the old sites of ABBEYVILLE and HILLERTON which have disappeared, to TAYLOR RESERVOIR.

A few miles north on a trail road are PIE PLANT MILL, DORCHESTER and BOWMAN, more ghost sites with only sagging shaft houses and brick foundations to show where prosperous mines and towns once stood. This road follows the old trail between the ARKANSAS VALLEY over TINCUP PASS, then over TAYLOR'S PASS to the north into

ASPEN.

TAYLOR RESERVOIR drains a large wilderness basin where deer, elk and bear hunting are good and the fishing and scenery superb. The road now swings south following rugged TAYLOR RIVER CANYON with its good fishing and camping sites.

At ALMONT, another former mining camp but now a fishing resort, the TAYLOR and the EAST RIVERS join to form the dashing GUNNISON RIVER. Follow State 135 to the town of GUNNISON (U. S. 50) eleven miles away.

GUNNISON divides its interests between catering to prosperous ranchers and to visitors, particularly fishermen, who come by the thousands during the summer for exciting vacations. It was named for Captain John Gunnison who was sent in 1856 to look for a practical railroad route to the Pacific coast.

WESTERN STATE COLLEGE has an excellent ARCHEOLOGICAL MUSEUM with outstanding examples of prehistoric Indian relics from the area.

Our By-Way tour now retraces State 135 following the frothy GUNNISON RIVER and the abandoned railroad grade back to ALMONT. Continuing on State 135 you pass JACK'S CABIN.

Next is CRESTED BUTTE at the foot of one of a series of peaks for which it is named. The town is unique because it was founded in 1879 when huge coal beds which vein the area were discovered. These same coal mines outlived the gold, silver, copper and lead strikes which boomed the surrounding region from time to time.

An interesting off-the-beaten-path trip leads straight north out of CRESTED BUTTE on a country road past the cemetery. This road climbs out of the valley around sharp hairpin curves, then clings precariously to the mountainside. From here you can see the few cabins remaining in GOTHIC built on a meadow and surrounded by high mountains with chalky cliffs. GOTHIC MOUNTAIN is to the east.

Some of the old cabins have been restored by members of the ROCKY MOUNTAIN BIOLOGICAL LABORATORY. This organization has a six-weeks school for field work in zoology, botany, and related sciences.

GOTHIC was founded in 1879 as a silver camp and General Grant visited it in 1880. For a real thrill rent some horses and ride up to ELKO and SCOFIELD and beyond to SCOFIELD PASS where they used to freight ore on muleback from ASPEN, less than 25 miles away as the crow flies. The sky-reaching ELK MOUNTAINS throw up a formidable barrier.

From CRESTED BUTTE State 135 angles west and climbs up KEBLER PASS (10,000 feet), then drops down through wild country threaded with sparkling trout streams. It crosses ANTHRACITE CREEK and turns west following this creek to where it joins MUDDY CREEK and becomes the North Fork of the GUNNISON RIVER.

At the road junction you may turn right and go straight north over MCCLURE PASS, then drop down into the rose-colored CRYSTAL RIVER VALLEY to REDSTONE, CARBONDALE, and ASPEN.

Our By-Way tour continues to the left on State 135 which widens and is paved from BOWIE through the fertile fruit orchards and farms which surround PAONIA and HOTCHKISS.

At HOTCHKISS you turn south on State 92. Just beyond CRAWFORD take the right hand fork and cross POISON MESA to the north rim of the BLACK CANYON OF THE GUNNISON. Here the shutterbug finds a challenge in the narrow dark walls squeezing together with the foaming river lashing and racing between them.

A scenic road parallels a portion of the north rim with nice picnic spots and imposing overlooks. You catch glimpses of the river boiling white with its miles of roaring water at a dizzying distance below. Do not attempt to descend into the CANYON without the Ranger's permission as it is very dangerous.

Return on the same road to State 92, then turn right swinging south then east across a corner of BLACK MESA, eventually joining U. S. 50 at BLUE MESA RESERVOIR.

You continue on U. S. 50 along the placid GUNNISON VALLEY, through GUNNISON.

Our By-Way tour continues via U. S. 50 through PARLIN, DOYLEVILLE, and SARGENTS over MONARCH PASS to SALIDA.

The Million Dollar Highway

By-Way Tour No. 2

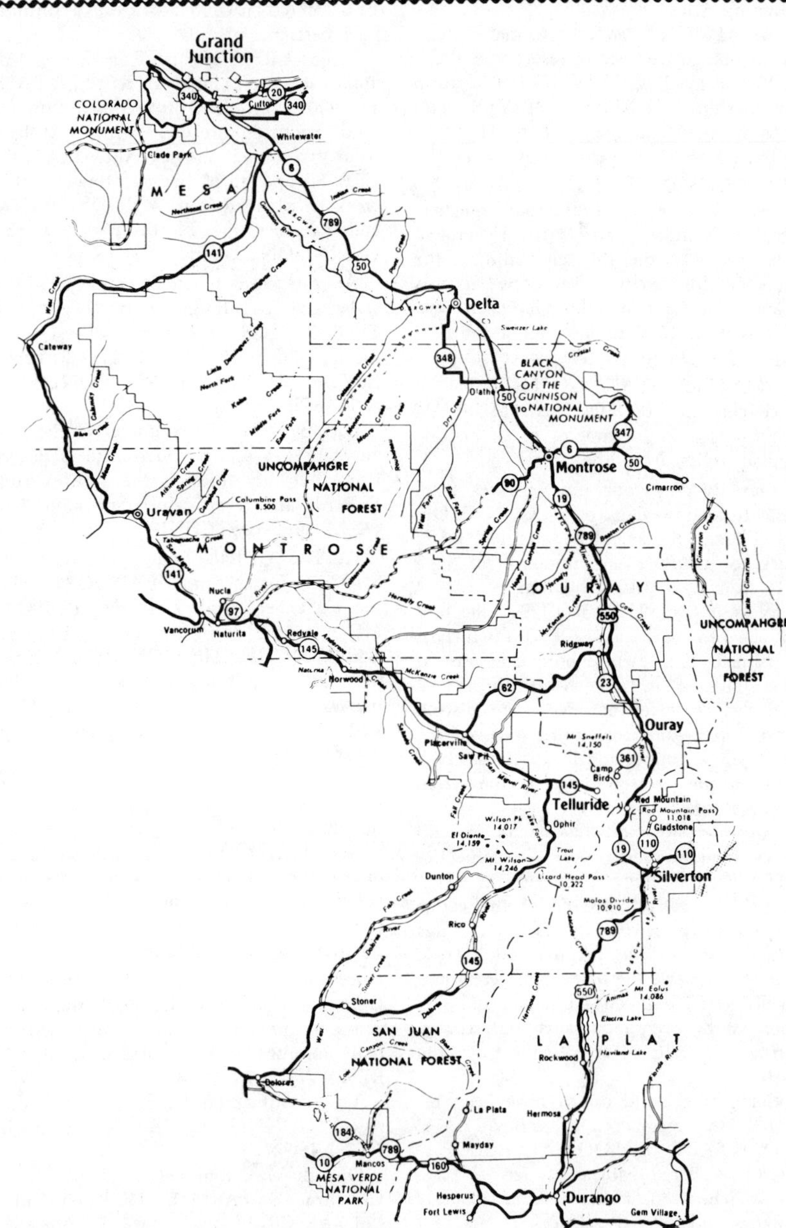

Often called the "American Alps," this region is the most rugged in the state with the "young" grey granite SAN JUAN mountain summits cut with sharp pinnacles and broken by awesome chasms. Here in this 100,000 square miles of spectacular scenery, there are 14 peaks which poke 14,000 feet skyward like massive fingers on some half-buried giant. Their fantastic splintered shapes, usually snow-crowned until July, rise from deep crevasses.

This country of beauty and jagged peaks was practically unknown except to Indians until late in the 19th Century when gold and silver were discovered in the "San Juan triangle" — actually a kite-shape — formed by LAKE CITY, OURAY, TELLURIDE and SILVER-TON whose very names set your imagination keeling. Over a half billion dollars in rich ore has been gouged from this area.

Our By-Way tour starts at bustling GRAND JUNCTION, hub of the great uranium boom after World War II. Situated at the entrance to the COLORADO PLATEAU (which extends into Utah, Arizona and New Mexico) fast-growing GRAND JUNCTION is the center of the Atomic Energy Commission for this region.

It's the largest city in COLORADO west of the CONTINENTAL DIVIDE and was founded in 1881 after the Utes were removed to their reservation in Utah. Irrigation was started almost immediately and with the coming of the DENVER & RIO GRANDE RAIL-ROAD in 1882, the small town grew rapidly.

GRAND JUNCTION has developed into the trading center for western COL-ORADO and eastern Utah, a large, sparsely populated area. The production of fine fruits — peaches, apricots, pears, cherries, grapes and plums has made GRAND JUNCTION and the GRAND VALLEY world-famous. The mild climate and long growing period encourage growing of grains and vegetables. Cattle and sheep thrive on the rich grasses.

Numerous parks dot the city and the fine new residential areas are built to take advantage of the views.

GRAND JUNCTION is also the center for a scenic vacationland.

You pick up U. S. 50 going southeast through DELTA to MONTROSE. This enterprising small town, founded in 1882 by Joseph Selig, is the seat of MONT-ROSE COUNTY. Once a thriving rail center on the narrow gauge during the hectic mining days, the town has now settled into a comfortable ranching, farming and vacation community.

An interesting side trip goes east out of MONTROSE 8 miles on U. S. 50, then turns north 6 miles on State 347 to the BLACK CANYON OF THE GUN-NISON NATIONAL MONUMENT.

The road follows the south rim with places to pause and gaze down into the awesome canyon, a shivering 2000 foot gorge with the white water GUNNI-SON RIVER at the bottom — a kind of mountain in reverse.

The BLACK CANYON was aptly described by the Indians as "the place of high rocks and much water." One of the most spectacular gorges in America, the canyon ranges in depth from 1730 to 2425 feet with brilliantly colored walls. But it is so narrow — the rims are sometimes only 1300 feet apart in places and 40 feet at the base — that the bottom of the gorge is usually quite dark except at midday. Hence the name, BLACK CANYON.

Our By-Way tour now returns to U.S. 50 and returns to MONTROSE.

Now you leave MONTROSE on U. S. 550 driving south through productive farm lands.

Right from the road is the UTE IN-DIAN MUSEUM which honors the illustrious Ute Chief Ouray and his beloved wife. This great Ute leader devoted most of his life to trying to keep peace between his people and the whites. Here is Chipeta's tomb as well as a concrete tepee built over a bubbling spring, and the only UTE INDIAN MUSEUM in COLO-RADO.

Straight ahead the majestic SAN JUANS throw a formidable barrier across the road, their sharp and twisted peaks a challenge to the visitor. The jagged 14,000 footer to the right is MT. SNEFFLES, cold as a winter's dawn, named for its resemblance to the fictional mountain in Jules Verne's "Mountains of the Moon."

The road follows the UNCOMPAH-GRE RIVER VALLEY which narrows into a rock gulch south of COLONA.

Beyond and just off the highway to the right is RIDGEWAY, once the terminal of the RIO GRANDE & SOUTHERN RAILROAD, a narrow gauge railroad which ran southwest from here to TELLURIDE, OPHIR, RICO and MANCOS. In later years it was known as the route of the "Galloping Goose."

U. S. 550 enters the UNCOMPAHGRE NATIONAL FOREST near PORTLAND where the UNCOMPAHGRE RIVER tumbles and cascades in foaming abandon between banks covered with lovely blue-grey fir forests.

HORSETHIEF TRAIL leading to the left was used by outlaws in early mining days to drive stolen horses to Utah and bring stolen cattle back. You may hike, jeep or ride horseback up the narrow trail to BRIDGE OF HEAVEN, a narrow hogback 2,000 feet above the canyon. The trail continues on to AMERICAN FLATS, a mesa, and follows the old road over the CONTINENTAL DIVIDE.

Several miles beyond this junction the stage-set town of OURAY appears in a cup of granite mountains with a sparkling backdrop of CASCADE FALLS spilling down the mountainside. Named for the Ute Chief, OURAY was founded in 1875 with the discovery of great silver lodes. Unrivaled for superb scenery, the small town lies in an alpine basin gazing up at multicolored mountain walls alternating red, grey, and even orange and purple shades, and surrounded by 12,000 to 13,000 foot peaks.

The town declined with the silver panic of 1893, but was revived when Tom Walsh discovered gold at the nearby CAMP BIRD MINE in 1896. Many kinds of minerals have been found here in paying quantity, but farming, ranching and tourists add to the economy.

The ornate HOTEL BEAUMONT, a rambling white brick, three-story building with its lofty ceilings and rosewood balcony, was the entertainment center during boom days. The gilded domed CITY HALL catches your eye at once. A heated swimming pool attracts visitors, and OURAY is a base for pack and jeep trips which will take you across glacial terrain and rocky canyons through primitive country with never-to-be-forgotten experiences.

Climbing out of OURAY on U. S. 550, just outside of town State 361 leads you west to BOX CANYON PARK. Follow a foot trail to BOX CANYON where CANYON CREEK WATERFALLS leap and plunge with such force that they have cut a fantastic narrow, rocky gash through solid rock, then the creek disappears in an underground passage. Another trail winds up to the HIGH BRIDGE spanning the creek.

At a fork in the road you drive up State 361, the backdoor road to CAMP BIRD MINE, discovered by Tom Walsh, an Irish-born carpenter, who made and lost a fortune before he came to OURAY in 1895. According to one story, Walsh was prospecting on the old GERTRUDE MINE property when he returned one noon to find his lunch stolen by "camp robbers" — large Rocky Mountain jays. He named his claim the CAMP BIRD and from it he eventually became a multimillionaire and an internationally-known figure. His daughter was Evalyn Walsh McLean of Hope Diamond fame.

Beyond CAMP BIRD is a trail leading to SNEFFLES, a ghost town, where the REVENUE TUNNEL, the RUBY TRUST, the ATLAS and the VIRGINIUS MINES are located. Over $27,000,000 in ore came out of here by 1919. There's a good ski area here now.

Back to U. S. 550, the highway climbs a steep hill with sharp switchbacks affording a magnificent view of OURAY below. You are now on the famous MILLION DOLLAR HIGHWAY, so-called because originally it was surfaced with gold-bearing gravels although their value was not known at the time. Actually the highway cost much more to build.

Otto Mears, who later built railroads into the area, literally hacked this first toll road out of the steep canyon and called it "The Rainbow Route." WHITE HOUSE MOUNTAIN to the right contrasts sharply with neighboring mountains. As you go through a tunnel, you get a dramatic view of MT. ABRAMS which looks like a pyramid. ENGINEER MOUNTAIN, one of the most photographed mountains in COLORADO, is to the left.

You'll want to pause at a parking area and gaze down at BEAR CREEK FALLS which slip from a canyon side and have a drop of 227 feet — twice the height of Niagara. Nearby is the bronze OTTO MEARS MEMORIAL TABLET dedicated to the "little giant" who built so many toll roads and three narrow gauge railroads in western COLORADO.

BEAR CREEK TRAIL takes off to the left of the highway following BEAR CREEK up past YELLOW JACKET MINE to AMERICAN FLATS where you can see OURAY cupped below. The GRAND MESA is to the north shadowed in the blue haze.

Our By-Way tour continues along U. S. 550 with sheer mountain cliffs on the left and the roaring, tumbling UNCOMPAHGRE RIVER hundreds of feet below. Prospect holes and mine dumps gopher the steep hills on either side of the canyon making you wonder how miners reached them before helicopters were invented. Gold and silver came "high" in these mountains.

Soon three stunning mountains appear to the left, each named RED MOUNTAIN. Iron ore has painted them a vivid hue. The MICKEY BREEN MINE is off to the left up POUGHKEEPSIE GULCH. Along the incredible shelf road, the mountains rear upward, steep and rugged. The highway goes around corkscrew curves climbing rapidly to IRONTON, founded in 1882, during the RED MOUNTAIN BOOM.

Most of the old houses at IRONTON have disappeared, as have those at GUSTON off the road to the left. But the tunnel entrances and drunken shaft houses mark where miners dug the ore.

The highway continues its dizzy climb with mines and shafts bleached to silver, lining either side of the canyon. When you come to a side road which takes off to the left it leads to the site of the old RED MOUNTAIN TOWN, located at the base of the incredible RED MOUNTAIN which might have come out of Dante's "Inferno." Nothing is left now except a few tumbledown shacks. A few rotted ties show where the railroad ran through the town. Skeletons of shaft houses show where the NATIONAL BELLE, the CONGRESS and the ENTERPRISE were located.

The "town" is as quiet today as it was loud and raucous during its hey-day when "the lights never went out in RED MOUNTAIN TOWN," while miners and gamblers elbowed each other and armed guards had to ride the ore trains to DURANGO and DENVER. A trail from here snakes east over the SAN JUANS and will take you either to LAKE CITY or CREEDE.

It's just a short distance now to the top of RED MOUNTAIN PASS which marks the boundary between the UNCOMPAHGRE and the SAN JUAN NATIONAL FORESTS. Now the highway drops down via wide switchbacks through heavy forests of pine, fir and spruce following MINERAL CREEK VALLEY.

At the foot of the pass is old CHATTANOOGA, discernible now, mainly by crumbling buildings and empty foundations.

The highway swings east now past the NORTH STAR SULTAN MINE, discovered in 1878, which has produced over $8,000,000 in ore. Hugging the side of a deep valley, the road descends to a little town whose atmosphere is distinctively Victorian. SILVERTON, built in 1874, appears below on a level mountain meadow completely mountain ringed.

Like a page out of "Currier and Ives," the village is the seat of SAN JUAN COUNTY, one of the few counties in the U. S. without an acre of assessed farming land. Isolated from the world by high mountains, the picturesque little town depends for livelihood on two

Early day Silverton

things — mining and tourists.

In its hey-day, three railroads spiraled metallic wealth down into the town's pockets. Now the fishermen and the atmosphere-hunting tourists bring a trickle of wealth up from the hot cities and prairies of the middlewest. The GRAND IMPERIAL HOTEL, built in 1883, has been faithfully restored to the Victorian period and contains an excellent museum. The old churches are most intriguing: the needle-spired white CONGREGATIONAL CHURCH is the oldest, built in 1881; the red brick ROMAN CATHOLIC CHURCH clings to a mountainside; and the rustic frame EPISCOPAL CHAPEL stands at the foot of ANVIL MOUNTAIN.

OLD BLAIR STREET is called "Movie Street" because so many movies have used it as a setting. Partially original, partially restored, the street will recall to you such pictures as "Across the Wide Missouri," "Denver & Rio Grande," "Ticket to Tomahawk," "Night Passage," "Maverick Queen," "Great Day in the Morning," "Run for Cover," and the railroad sequence in "Around the World in 80 Days."

An interesting side trip is to drive a short distance northeast, then take the road up CEMENT CREEK to GLADSTONE, site of the GOLD KING MILL. Most of the buildings have disappeared and the tracks of Otto Mears' SILVERTON, GLADSTONE & NORTHERLY narrow gauge have been ripped up, but you can see the old roadbed. A trail leads on to RED MOUNTAIN.

Back to the main road, you again drive northeast past the SHENANDOAH-DIVES MILL. You've probably heard the figure of speech — "pie in the sky." Well, here it actually came true. Above to the right you'll see the aerial tramway which carried the miners daily to the SHENANDOAH MINES high on the mountainside. The old boarding house, across from the mine, was also reached by another tram. Every ounce of food, supplies and all the manpower was carried up on this tram, while on its return trip, the tram brought ore down to the mill. Thus, the miners had "pie in the sky" every day.

HOWARDSVILLE was the first county

Denver and Rio Grande's famous Narrow Gauge train on the "high line" in the Animas Gorge

seat and the old log courthouse still stands.

Continuing along the road from HOW-ARDSVILLE, you come to EUREKA where the gigantic SUNNYSIDE MILL spread itself down almost the whole mountainside. It has been torn down, unfortunately, but what a sight it was. A few more miles will take you to ANI-MAS FORKS where the GOLD PRINCE MINE reigned. Trails lead to various mines and the interesting ghost sites of MINERAL POINT, ENGINEER CITY or to ROSE'S CABIN enroute to LAKE CITY. Another trail leads straight east via CINNAMON PASS to WHITE CROSS (ghost town) and on to LAKE CITY. You must retrace your steps to SILVERTON along this road which Otto Mears built first as a toll road, then on top of it he built the SILVERTON NORTHERN RAILROAD, completed in 1896.

Back at SILVERTON be sure to visit the old COURTHOUSE. Outside is a large marker with samples of ore from dozens of mines in the vicinity.

You pick up U. S. 550 again, following the South Fork of the ANIMAS RIVER — named by the Spaniards "El Rio de las Animas Perdidas" meaning "The River of Lost Souls" because it was so treacherous and many persons drowned while trying to ford it. Next you climb up a series of hairpin curves leaving the river. Be sure to stop and look back at SILVERTON sitting placidly against its theatrical backdrop on its high mountain meadow, dreaming of past glory.

Engine 476 ready to leave the station

Now you cross MOLAS DIVIDE, entering SAN JUAN NATIONAL FOREST. To the right is GRAND TURK MOUNTAIN and to the left are the spectacular NEEDLE MOUNTAINS — highest square mile in the nation — and the roughest of the rough mountains in the SAN JUANS.

Dropping down into LIME CREEK VALLEY, you'll see ENGINEER MOUNTAIN rearing off to the right. Next is LIME CREEK BURN which shows the tragic remains of a forest fire in 1878. Be careful! Put out your fires!

To the right are the multi-colored HERMOSA CLIFFS. Nearby PURGATORY SKI RESORT is southern COLORADO'S largest. To the left is ELECTRA LAKE, and beyond is HAVILAND LAKE. Near ROCKWOOD, an old-time lumber camp, the highway crosses the D & RG tracks and drops down into the ANIMAS VALLEY. The river, the railroad and the highway run parallel now.

DURANGO is known as the "Narrow Gauge Capital of the World" because here the visitor may board the only regularly scheduled narrow gauge railroad, the D & RG, and ride through ANIMAS CANYON to SILVERTON (you will find there is no road or trail on part of this route because the canyon is too narrow in spots for more than one roadbed).

Leave your car at the railroad station and take the train for an all-day excursion. You'll be at once enchanted by this picturesque railroad which still uses the old-time coaches and tiny engines. You wonder if they'll ever "make the grade." The railroad follows ANIMAS VALLEY for several miles, then winds up on a shelf blasted out of solid rock several hundred feet above the rushing river. You are suddenly transported into a breathtaking experience as the train cliff-hugs the canyon wall. It's like another world as you gaze down into the squirming, foaming river below.

Now the train snakes down into the valley and follows the river. No shutter-bug who has ever used color film will want to miss this experience. TACOMA is the Western Colorado Power Co. plant getting water from ELECTRA LAKE. Ah Wilderness! is a dude ranch. Movies are made along this theatrical route. Now the craggy NEEDLE MOUNTAINS appear to the right giving the shutterbug a real workout.

Stops are made en route to let off fishermen who will fish along the river all day, then catch the train when it returns in the afternoon. Supplies are unloaded for ranchers and miners. Usually the passengers pitch in and help the crew unload.

NEEDLETON was once a mining camp and now caters to tourists. You'll see evidence of snowslides along the canyon and places where the tracks have been moved and rebuilt. ELK PARK is named for those beautiful animals who winter here. Often the train crews bring hay for them when the snow is deep since elks' hoofs are not sharp like the deers' and they cannot dig in snow for their forage.

You eat lunch in SILVERTON and spend a couple of hours exploring, taking pictures — if you're lucky, there will be a little shower and when the sun comes out again you may get some color shots of a rainbow. The train leaves at 2:40 and returns through the same scenic canyon to DURANGO.

Our By-way tour turns west from DURANGO to MANCOS, then takes State 184 which follows the RIO GRANDE AND SOUTHERN railroad grade to DOLORES. Here you turn northeast on State 145 through RICO, O P H I R, TELLURIDE to PLACER-VILLE. (This route is discussed in detail in By-Way Tour No. 7 in this volume.)

Now you turn northeast and continue on State 145 through NORWOOD, and REDVALE to NATURITA.

NATURITA was once a small village of western false-front stores. The uranium boom has changed this. Now there are neon lights and plenty of glass fronts since the Vanadium Co. of America built its uranium mill here. The first atomic bomb was made from uranium produced in MONTROSE COUNTY.

You may continue northwest to URA-VAN where the Union Carbide Nuclear Mill processes the carnotite (yellow ore) which yields uranium and vanadium. First discovered here in 1881 in combination with gold, it wasn't until 1898 that uranium's value as a source of radioactive material was recognized after Madame Curie used some of their ore in the discovery of radium.

Now the highway crosses the eastern side of PARADOX VALLEY, named because the DOLORES RIVER perversely seems to run the wrong way. This is weirdly beautiful desert country in shades of red, yellow and buff supporting only sagebrush, rabbit brush and a few cacti. Believed to be the bed of an ancient sea there are salt mines which the uranium mills exploit for their use.

From BEDROCK the adventurous vacationist may want to hire a guide and explore rugged DOLORES CANYON to the south. Cattle raising and some farming appear along PARADOX CREEK to PARADOX.

PARADOX has also boomed with the uranium discoveries. One road turns south, climbs the cedar-studded NYS-WONGER MESA and angles through the desert to Moab, Utah. Long vistas spread before you with the plateau dropping off in steps toward the COLORA-DO RIVER. In the distance are the La Sal Mountains in Utah, a purple smudge on the horizon. Here the whole earth can shimmer with eye-blinding heat under burning turquoise skies or shiver under chill desert winds.

State 141 continues northwest from URAVAN following the DOLORES RIVER to GATEWAY, another uranium center. Now it's only 45 miles northeast to GRAND JUNCTION.

A short side trip from NATURITA is straight north on State 97 to NUCLA, a village started by an interesting co-operative venture where everyone earned and shared alike. Human nature being what it is, this cooperative experiment finally dissolved with only the handmade irrigation ditch continuing as community property. NUCLA remained a small village of tidy cottages resisting change until the advent of the Geiger counter and the discovery of uranium. Now it too has changed. A country road cuts diagonally a c r o s s UNCOMPAHGRE PLATEAU to DELTA, 53 miles away.

Our By-Way tour takes State 90 northeast from NATURITA climbing up UN-COMPAHGRE PLATEAU, s p a r s e l y sprinkled with scrub oak and cedar. Then it drops down into the UNCOM-PAHGRE VALLEY and returns to MONTROSE.

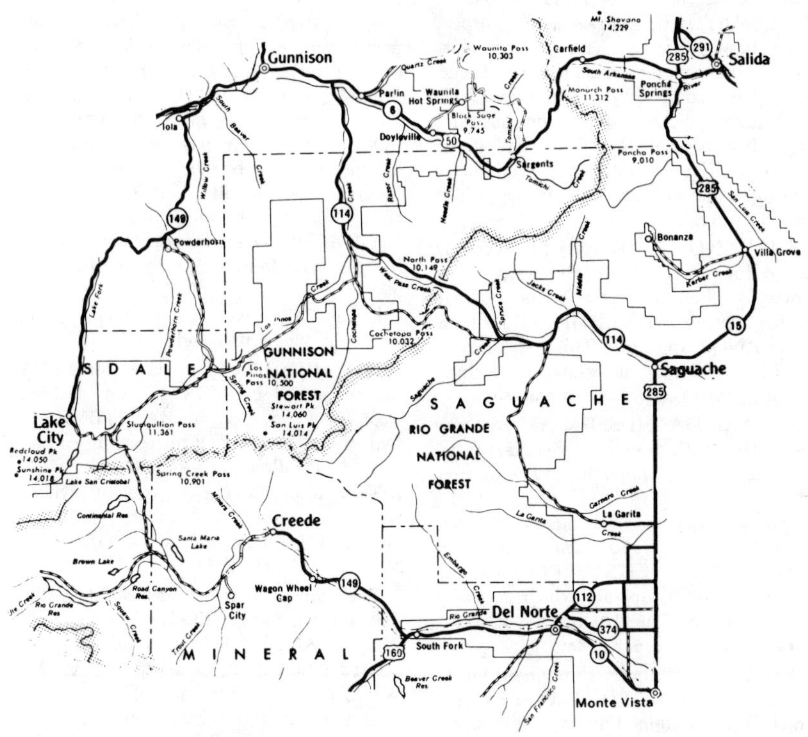

Roads that meander in and out of two National Forests through vast stretches of virgin forest, that cover millions of acres in the almost untouched mountains of southwestern COLORADO, that stick close to trout streams and high-altitude lakes, that stir haunting memories of the tales of early mining days and Indian troubles, and that climb the backbone of two mountain ranges are the object of this By-Way tour.

The Ute Indians claimed this country and fought bitterly to hold it even after gold and silver were discovered.

Most of our route lies above 6000 feet in altitude with high spots going above timberline for the visitor who wants to do some real exploring. Today's goals are CREEDE and LAKE CITY whose very names conjure up nostalgic interest in the violent tales of mining camps of another century.

Our By-Way tour starts at SALIDA (U. S. 285 & 50), founded in the 1880's by the DENVER & RIO GRANDE. The railroad was pushing its narrow gauge tracks to booming LEADVILLE and building another line over the CONTINENTAL DIVIDE and down the GUNNISON VALLEY to GRAND JUNCTION.

SALIDA calls itself the "Heart of the Rockies." It is certainly the center of mineral country with almost as wide a variety of minerals, ores and rocks as is found anywhere in the state. The rockhound will find a bonanza here.

At the north edge of town a county road leads northeast four miles to the SEDALIA COPPER MINE where huge almandite garnet crystals are found as well as several other minerals. Beyond is TURRET, a ghost town, built up against the mountain. Gold was mined here and at nearby WHITEHORN as the crooked shaft houses and prospect holes show. Nice gem sapphires, garnets, epidote and sagenite specimen are found in the pegmatite dikes. The huge feldspar quarry yielded quartz crystals and mica. Just beyond is CALUMET which produced iron in quantities, and here, too, are found epidote, garnets, sapphires, and sagenite.

SHAVANO PEAK to the west is named for a Ute Chief and means "blue flower." When the snow starts to melt in the spring the ANGEL OF THE SHAVANO appears. This spectacular angel-like outline of snow is formed in the crevices on the mountainside.

The SALIDA MUSEUM (U. S. 50) has a fine collection of Indian artifacts, historical items, minerals and old firearms.

Our By-Way tour swings west from SALIDA on U. S. 50, then turns south abruptly at PONCHA SPRINGS. The Utes knew the 99 springs which gave the area its name. The JACKSON HOTEL dates back to the early days.

The highway climbs through a lovely wooded canyon to PONCHA PASS over which Lt. Zebulon Pike and his party struggled through waist-deep snow in 1806. Beyond you can still trace the abandoned narrow gauge railroad grade.

Now the spectacular west side of the SANGRE DE CRISTOS (Blood of Christ) parallels the highway to the east. The lower SAWATCH RANGE is to the west, and the level SAN LUIS VALLEY fans out to the south, an incredibly level tableland hemmed in by gigantic mountains.

VILLA GROVE has always been a supply center from its earliest days. West from the little hamlet along KERBER CREEK are the ghost towns of CLAYTONIA, BONITA, SEDGEWICK, KERBER CITY, BONANZA, and EXCHEQUERVILLE. Once they were gold and silver camps. Good ore and mineral specimen may be found here.

Two-and-one-half miles north of VILLA GROVE and about five miles northwest is the HALL TURQUOISE MINE where turquoise matrix can still be found in the dumps.

Now highway 285 swings sharply to the southwest and into SAGUACHE (blue water), a typical western ranch town where you'll see more blue levis, ten-gallon hats and high-heeled boots than any other type of clothes. Today the town drowses in the summer sun or resposes quietly under winter snows. Ranches are today's basis for prosperity. But it had a lively past during the days of the mining booms and when Otto Mears, the railroad giant of the SAN JUAN, started building his toll road. SAGUACHE was also the headquarters for the Ute Indian Agency in the early days.

U. S. 285 leaves SAGUACHE going south on the "gunbarrel" highway.

Near CENTER you take State 112 southwest to DEL NORTE, then continue west on U. S. 160 to BAXTERVILLE. Our By-Way tour turns northwest on State 159 following the RIO GRANDE RIVER along a narrow canyon whose sides are covered with cedar, pinon and pine, and enters the RIO GRANDE NATIONAL FOREST.

The canyon narrows and so does the road until it nudges the bank of the roily RIO GRANDE. This narrow, brightly-colored canyon is called WAGON WHEEL GAP because of a broken wagon wheel and other belongings scattered along the trail by a party of pioneers who were chased out of the country by the Utes.

The village is also called WAGON WHEEL GAP. Many palatial summer estates dot the area.

For the person who wants a trip into real "back country," a horseback trip with a guide may be arranged to WHEELER NATIONAL MONUMENT in the LA GARITA MOUNTAINS to the north. The trail follows BELLOWS CREEK for about 15 miles. The monument's 60 acres of eroded sandstone is literally "out of this world."

This wonderland of nature, a great volcanic upheaval, is tucked away near the sky. Called a "parade of ghosts," the area is a conglomeration of sculptured spooks, camel humps, a pig and a potato rock, fantastic ramparts, a garden of

The Angel of Mt. Shavano spreads her arms to the Heavens

gnomes, nooks and crannies, lost caverns, and balanced rocks.

Colors vary from stark white, through greyish white, yellow to salmon pink. The Indians regarded it with awe and avoided it as a "never-never" land. The return trip may be made via CREEDE.

Beyond WAGON WHEEL GAP is CREEDE which takes its place alongside of CRIPPLE CREEK, CENTRAL CITY, ASPEN, LEADVILLE, SILVERTON and OURAY as a famous mining camp where millions of dollars in gold and silver were mined. In the '70's a trail led through this region enroute to SILVERTON and OURAY during the SAN JUAN fever. But it wasn't until N. C. Creede discovered "color" in 1890 that the country boomed. He named his mine the HOLY MOSES. The discovery of the KING SOLOMON MINES brought thousands of miners rushing headlong into the district, and CREEDE became a rowdy mining camp.

"It's day all day in the daytime, and there is no night in Creede," painted a true picture of the wild boom town. Floods down the RIO GRANDE and fire have changed CREEDE'S face many times, but a few landmarks still stand. One of the best known is FORD'S SALOON built by the notorious Bob Ford who is supposed to have shot Jesse James.

CREEDE folded in the 1893 silver panic, but there have been sporadic revivals and certain properties are worked from time to time. But more than this, CREEDE is the gateway to a romantic past which will never be revived.

There's very little left of BACHELOR, about three miles north of CREEDE, where the LAST CHANCE MINE paid off to the tune of $170 per ton. The KING SOLOMON MINE, later called the AMETHYST, and the CLEOPATRA, the COMMODORE, and the DEL MONTE contributed their share to the bonanza. Fossils are found in the surrounding hills.

Green and blue turquoise may be found near the AMETHYST and COMMODORE MINES. In addition, amethyst is found on most of the mine dumps on BACHELOR MOUNTAIN, particularly at the AMETHYST MINE.

On the other side of the mountain was SUNNYSIDE now reached from CREEDE on a trail road to the right about three miles south of town. The old mine dumps spilling down the hillsides once belonged to such famous paying properties as the KREUTZE, the SONATA, the CORSAIR, and the YELLOW JACK.

From CREEDE to LAKE CITY over SLUMGULLION PASS is one of the most thrilling auto trips in COLORADO due to its remoteness, scenic beauty, real wilderness area, and good fishing in clear streams. Summer is a delightful time to take this trip (the pass is closed in the winter), but for a real show take the trip in the autumn when the aspens have turned to gold. Scarlet scrub oak and other highly colored bushes give the mountainside the appearance of being spread with multicolored oriental carpets. The blue, blue sky takes on an intensity contrasting with the shimmering yellow aspen which is a breathtaking sight.

State 149 swings southwest out of CREEDE past ANTLERS PARK to SEVEN-MILE BRIDGE. The left hand road goes up LIME CREEK to SPAR CITY, another ghost town. Our By-Way tour continues on State 149 which parallels the RIO GRANDE RIVER, making a deep V, turning northwest. From here on the natural beauty of the country is almost overwhelming.

A reminder of Colorado's fabulous gold rush days

At a road junction the adventurous visitor may want to follow the road to the left up to the RIO GRANDE RESERVOIR at the base of RIO GRANDE PRYAMID, a mountain which is usually snow-covered.

A horseback and jeep trail leads through the ghost towns of JUNCTION CITY and BEARTOWN, then over old STONY PASS to SILVERTON on the other side of the rugged SAN JUANS. Another trail swings north along LOST TRAIL CREEK to CARSON (ghost town), over old CINNAMON PASS to OURAY or straight north to LAKE CITY. You are now in high country, often above timberline. Brilliant alpine flowers — tiny blue forget-me-nots, purple sky pilots, alpine gold-flowers, and many others, dot the tundra.

Our By-Way tour stays on the highway and now leaves the RIO GRANDE, turning straight north across a lovely forested mesa and crosses SOUTH FORK CREEK. To the left, off the highway, the icy stream plunges down three beautiful high falls with rainbow and cutthroat trout lurking in the pools below. Little pink elephant flowers and blue chiming bells grow profusely along the creek banks.

A few miles beyond is SPRING CREEK PASS which offers a sweeping panorama of the sharp SAN JUANS looming jagged and blue.

When the highway reaches a junction, you turn left and start climbing up through pine and aspen forests, snaking around thrilling hairpin curves to the top of SLUMGULLION PASS, named for the stew which the miners made as they paused en route to the gold fields.

To the northwest jagged UNCOMPAHGRE PEAK cuts the horizon. The irregular SAN JUANS seem an almost insurpassable barrier to the west. As you drop down off the pass, you catch glimpses of lovely SAN CRISTOBEL LAKE. At the foot of the pass is a grave where five men are buried, victims of Alfred Packer who killed them in 1873. Nearby CANNIBAL PLATEAU is named for the gruesome story.

At the road junction, you may take the left hand one past the lake (good fishing), following the GUNNISON RIVER to SHERMAN, a ghost town which is still pretty well preserved. Beyond along a thin trail are WHITE-CROSS, TELLURIUM and ANIMAS FORKS which have practically disappeared. The producing mines were the CHAMPION, the CRACKER JACK, the BONHOMME, and the TOBASCO. The mine dumps yield interesting ore specimen for those persons willing to make the trip.

Throughout this drive you will be impressed with the bigness and the loneliness of this country — the immensity of land and sky, the huge mountains, the wide meadows, the deep canyons, and the blue sky forming a vast canopy overhead. Occasional flocks of sheep on summer pasture are seen.

Our By-Way tour continues north on State 149 to LAKE CITY, laid out in 1875, and one of the most charming mining towns in the state. Wide cottonwood-lined streets bordered with bluish stone buildings and turn-of-the-century houses with plenty of "gingerbread" have withstood the ravages of time. Occasional brick foundations and gaps between the buildings show where fire has taken its toll. The tiny Victorian churches look like picture post cards.

The seat of HINSDALE COUNTY, LAKE CITY, too, had its boom and bust times. Today it lives most of the year in blissful peace and isolation, coming to life in the summer when visitors by the thousands come here for a never-to-be-forgotten vacation among its lakes, forests, streams and ghost towns.

A good side trip leads straight west out of LAKE CITY up HENSEN GULCH. Your auto can make it as far as HENSEN. Beyond that it is best to take horses or a jeep. At first the trail follows the creek then winds up past the HIDDEN TREASURE, the UTE-ULAY and the OCEAN WAVE mines with their drunken-looking shaft houses, crumbling foundations and colorful mine dumps. Good ore specimen are there for the taking.

Beyond is CAPITAL CITY, a real ghost town, with a few buildings standing, although after each winter's storms some disappear. About five miles farther is ROSE'S CABIN, once a popular overnight stopping place on the CONTINENTAL DIVIDE en route to OURAY. Another trail leads south from here to ANIMAS FORKS, then over STONY PASS to SILVERTON.

Our By-Way tour leaves LAKE CITY and continues north on State 149 following the Lake Fork of the GUNNISON RIVER. To the west is UNCOMPAHGRE NATIONAL FOREST and the scarred SAN JUANS with their heads often in the clouds. It's a region of numerous ranches.

At GATEVIEW the road swings east leaving the GUNNISON RIVER and winding up on SAPINERO MESA covered with scrub oak, sage and junipers.

Off the road a mile is POWDERHORN, with CEBOLLA HOT SPRINGS which the Ute Indians knew well.

Now the highway swings north through CEBOLLA VALLEY. To the left one mile is SPENCER, another ghost town, where the HEADLIGHT, the OLD LOTT, and the ANACONDA once flourished. It's just a few miles across the fertile GUNNISON VALLEY to IOLA (U. S. 50).

Our By-Way tour turns east on U. S. 50 through GUNNISON.

You will continue east on U. S. 50 along TOMICHI CREEK to State 114 which turns south just before getting to PARLIN.

An alternate road is to continue on U. S. 50 over MONARCH PASS to SALIDA.

Our By-Way tour turns south on State 114 on what, in the early days, was known as "SAGUACHE ROAD." It follows COCHETOPA CREEK through a fertile farming and ranching region to where ARCHULETA CREEK empties into COCHETOPA.

Now the road swings east, climbing up through stands of pine, spruce and aspen to COCHETOPA PASS, a low saddle over the CONTINENTAL DIVIDE.

Historic COCHETOPA PASS was first used by the Indians, later by the Spanish explorers, followed by the French fur traders in 1837. There was a Mormon Trail here in 1847 en route to Utah, and in 1853 Captain John W. Gunnison, looking for a good railroad route to the Pacific, crossed the pass. This is also wilderness country excellent for fishing and big game hunting. You'll see many flocks of sheep in summer pasture high on the mountainsides.

A few miles below is SAGUACHE and from here you will retrace your route turning east, then north over PONCHA PASS and back to SALIDA.

Great Sand Dunes and Cumbres Pass

By-Way Tour No. 4

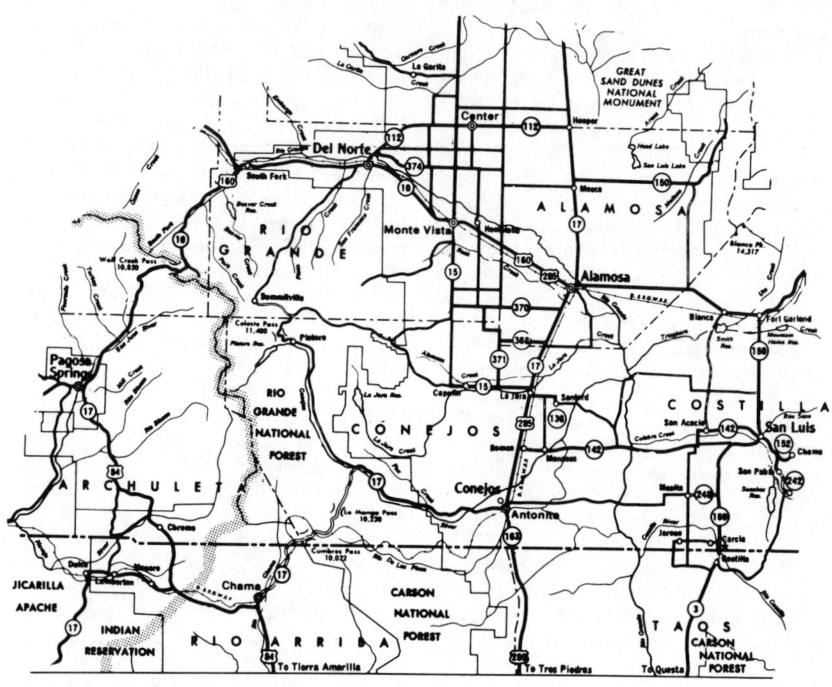

America's roof garden is the name which best describes the SAN LUIS VALLEY since it is the highest agricultural district in the country. The largest of the four great COLORADO mountain parks, the valley is a dry, inland floor 100 miles long, 60 miles wide and its elevation is 7500 feet above sea level.

Picturesque high mountains encompass the valley like giant parentheses. As you gaze across the valley you get an acute sense of vastness. First are the verdant acres of irrigated crops — red McClure potatoes, cabbages, head lettuce, cauliflower, garden peas, sugar beets, Moravian barley and lush alfalfa. Beyond is the endless roll of plains gray with sagebrush, chalky-white with alkali and sparkling with 1500 artesian wells shooting their life-giving water skyward. These wells are beautiful any time of year, but they are spectacular in the winter when they look like great frozen fountains or inverted icicles flashing rainbows of light in the bright sun.

The SAN LUIS VALLEY is surrounded by a gigantic playground for vacationers. Throughout the mountain areas there is excellent fishing and hunting, hiking, mountain climbing, rockhounding, picnicking, camping and dude ranches with packing-in facilities. Any town in the valley is less than thirty minutes from some colorful recreational area.

Our By-Way tour starts at ALAMOSA (cottonwood grove), the largest town in the valley which was founded in 1878 when the D&RG was building west to DURANGO. It went through the usual growing pains of a "wild west" railroad town complete with saloons, dancehalls, lynchings, gamblers, and prospectors enroute to the gold and silver camps in the "silvery SAN JUANS."

Today the small city is a thriving agricultural and stock center shipping thousands of carloads of the famous red McClure potatoes all over the country as well as truck vegetables and Moravian barley for the Coors Brewery in GOLDEN, COLORADO. Hereford and Angus cattle and clover-fed sheep are prime commodities. ADAMS STATE COLLEGE is located on the west side of town.

During the summer excursions leave the ALAMOSA depot on the CUMBRES & TOLTEC RAILROAD, one of the few remaining narrow gauge railroads in the country. It's an exciting and picturesque trip through TOLTEC GORGE (no auto roads), over scenic CUMBRES PASS, and down to Chama, New Mexico. The railroad is owned jointly by the states of COLORADO and New MEXICO.

Our By-Way tour turns south out of ALAMOSA on U.S. 285. This valley is farmed when irrigation water is available.

LA JARA is noted for garden peas, although many other vegetables are raised and shipped from here as well as stock. About five miles east on State 136 is SANFORD, first known as EPHRAIM, founded in 1880 by the Mormons.

Continuing on U. S. 285, you go through ROMEO, another farming community. A few miles beyond a black-topped road leads to the right one mile to CONEJOS (rabbit), seat of CONEJOS COUNTY. One of the earliest towns in COLORADO, CONEJOS was founded in 1854. The courthouse still contains old records, many in Spanish and dating back to the Mexican and Spanish colonial days. OUR LADY of GUADALUPE CHURCH of Spanish Mission design is the oldest Roman Catholic Church in COLORADO, built in 1856. The historic MAJOR LAFAYETTE HEAD HOUSE is the long low adobe building north of the courthouse.

Back on U. S. 285 you continue to ANTONITO, last town of any size in the valley and an important shipping, lumber and vacation center.

Tall columns of white smoke identify nearby lumber mills while long wooden sheds line the railroad tracks to house produce for shipping. About five miles south of town U.S. 285 enters New Mexico continuing to Espanola and Santa Fe. A trip like this is a neat and foolproof way to bring out the Tom Sawyer and Huck Finn that lurks in everyone.

Our By-Way tour leaves U.S. 285 at ANTONITO and turns west following State 17 through MOGATE and LAS MESITAS. Both are Spanish-American hamlets or placitas (little plazas), as are CANON, ORTIZ, LOS PINOS and SAN MIGUEL off the road to the south.

These tiny villages are interesting to visit, with their friendly people always ready to do you a favor. The drab brown and tan adobe houses are dressed up with strings of bright red chili peppers hanging from the roofs or vegas (rafters). The door and window frames are often painted in Virgin's blue to keep out evil spirits. You have entered a region where time, if it has not stood still, has at least slowed down and allowed the country to retain its memorable charm.

The only art indigenous to America was developed along this upper RIO GRANDE VALLEY and on south to Santa Fe between 1750 and 1850. For almost 100 years these people were isolated from Mexico and Spain during a period of turbulent history in those countries. The Roman Catholic Church was the only Christian church in the region, and they, too, lost touch for various reasons. The natives, a devout and superstitious people, kept alive what they could of the church beliefs and customs. From this developed the santos (saints) made by native artists. Two kinds existed: bultos (handcarved figures) and reredos (carved and painted wall placques). All the old churches and practically every home had either one or both on their altars. Today these santos are collectors' items and most have gone into museums and private collections, although some of the churches still retain them.

The Penitente Order, a lay group, was responsible for many of the church services. Some of their moradas (tiny adobe churches, often without a window) still stand and are used particularly during Passion Week (no visitors). Crude wooden crosses seen along the road identify the trail taken by the Penitente Brothers.

Back on the highway you are following the cool, sparkling CONEJOS RIVER, usually shallow enough to wade across in midsummer, but a raging torrent in the spring when the snow starts melting on the high peaks. Willows and narrow-leaf cottonwoods march along the banks.

At a road junction you leave the beaten path following the CONEJOS RIVER along a rebuilt mine toll road to PLATORO RESERVOIR at the base of MONTEZUMA PEAK. Besides good fishing and hunting country, rockhounds will enjoy the area. PLATORO was founded in the '80's when rich gold ore was discovered here and at SUMMITVILLE. The original PLATORO is now a ghost town, but there are cabins for vacationers. The town was revived in 1901 by another gold and silver strike. The PAROLE and MAMMOTH MINE dumps yield nice specimen.

Ore was discovered at the GILMORE MINE on KLONDYKE MOUNTAIN, a couple of miles west of PLATORO in 1913 and again the little village came to life. But the boom was short-lived. Now a shelf road twists around the mountain and below against some red cliffs you can see all that is left of STUNNER — weed-choked foundations — where gold was found in 1879. Old mine tailings show where the SNOW STORM, the LOG CABIN, the EURYDICE and the MERRIMAC paid off.

Continuing a few miles, the shelf road forks. The left hand road follows WIGHTMAN FORK CREEK climbing a series of narrow switchbacks to SUMMITVILLE where gold was discovered in 1871. The LITTLE ANNIE was the biggest producer. Mining is still done in this area and new houses have replaced the old ghost town. You may take a well-graded road which follows PINOS CREEK northeast into DEL NORTE, 21 miles away. Or you may retrace your steps to the forks, then turn east to JASPAR, which has changed from a ghost to a resort town. A well-graded road leads east, dividing and going into LA JARA or ALAMOSA or north into MONTE VISTA.

Our By-Way tour stays on State 17 making a sharp left turn and leaving the CONEJOS RIVER, climbing LA MANGA PASS.

The beautiful winding paved road follows the old ARCHULETA TOLL ROAD, named for a Spanish explorer of the 17th Century. There are spectacular views as you round each curve. In the summer red beardstongue, purple vetch, salmon cowboy's delight, scarlet Indian paintbrush, and blue harebells brighten fields and narrow canyons, making a truly colorful scene.

In the autumn this is one of the most beautiful drives in COLORADO with golden aspen quivering in the sunlight like tongues of yellow flame against the dark spruce and fir. While hillsides are carpeted in a multitude of colors as frost tints the scrub oak, berry and mountain mahogany bushes in a variety of red, orange and yellow, are accented by a turquoise sky.

After topping CUMBRES PASS you meet the tracks of the railroad which has followed another valley. A wye protected by drab wooded snowsheds reminds you that deep snowdrifts are treacherous up here during the winter. During the summer if you are lucky, you'll see the narrow gauge train puffing its tortuous way up the pass with a tiny "helper" engine pushing vigorously from the rear behind the miniature caboose.

A few miles away APACHE LAKE sits on top of the CONTINENTAL DIVIDE and spills its waters to both the Atlantic and Pacific watersheds. Because of this, the Apache Indians still consider this lake a holy place and even today some of the older men come for secret rites.

Now State 17 crosses the State line where it becomes New Mexico State 17. The highway drops down rapidly to the CHAMA RIVER VALLEY where you cross the river and abruptly you are in the village of CHAMA. Predominantly Spanish-American, the sleepy little town's main street looks like a set from a TV Western with its false-front stores. The old grey railroad station and yards with the black coal shutes are on another level down near the river. CHAMA ships many cattle, sheep and much lumber.

Here you could pick up U.S. 84. Going south the highway would take you through colorful CHAMA CANYON to Espanola and Santa Fe.

Our By-Way tour turns west, then north on U. S. 84 crossing the CONTINENTAL DIVIDE. This is part of the old Mexican TIERRA AMARILLA (yellow earth) LAND GRANT.

State 17 leads west to MONERO, LUMBERTON and DULCE, the latter headquarters for the APACHE JICARILLA RESERVATION. During the summer the Apaches hold some picturesque Indian dances here.

Our By-Way tour continues northwest on U. S. 84 crossing the Colorado-New Mexico State line to CHROMO (color). Mountain mahogany, sagebrush and cliff roses are making a slow comeback in the arroyos where overgrazing brought about serious erosion. Deep canyons testify to the abuse. This is wild, desolate country bordering the Indian reservation where those people were pushed last century.

You now join U. S. 160 at PAGOSA SPRINGS (discussed in By-Way Tour No. 5). Now the highway curves north climbing rapidly up WOLF CREEK CANYON. Off the road along tiny creeks little pink elephants (elephantellas), blue climbing bells (mertensia) and other dainty mountain flowers grow on the mossy banks. The rockhound should search along WOLF CREEK, particularly close to the top of the pass, for agate nodules with white quartz crystals, and moonstones.

WOLF CREEK PASS crosses the CONTINENTAL DIVIDE at 10,850 feet. There's a good ski center here with tow. Straight south of the pass is TREASURE MOUNTAIN (foot trail only), where there is supposed to be 33 million dollars in gold bricks hidden on the mountainside. Cached here in the 18th Century by a group of Frenchmen, the treasure has been sought by many parties but no trace has ever been found.

Our By-Way tour makes a rapid descent down the steep pass which is the boundary between the SAN JUAN and RIO GRANDE NATIONAL FORESTS.

At SOUTH FORK the creek empties into the RIO GRANDE. Now the road starts across dry sage flats, the beginning of the SAN LUIS VALLEY with only a few cottonwoods and willows showing where the streams are.

For an off-the-beaten-path trail take the country road leading north from GRANGER (U. S. 160) following EMBARGO CREEK. There's good fishing along the clear streams. The rockhound will find many old mine dumps to explore en route to the ghost town sites of EMBARGO and SKY CITY, which are at the head of the creek.

Continuing on U. S. 160 you reach DEL NORTE, which was founded in 1860 as a stopping place for wagon trains en route to the gold fields in the SAN JUANS. Some of the old stone buildings still stand. You can make your own soda pop from the well in the center of town by adding it to your lemonade. The town is now a ranching, farming and tourist center.

About ten miles northwest of DEL NORTE at the western edge of the valley the rockhound will find good specimens of banded agate, chalcedony, white opal, quartz crystals, jasperized lava and geodes.

Our By-Way tour continues east on U. S. 160 through fertile green irrigated fields. MONTE VISTA (mountain view) is aptly named because you can see the mountains in every direction. The SKI-HIGH STAMPEDE held here every July is a real western rodeo complete with bronco busting, calf roping and riding vicious Brahma steers. Although reminiscent of the Old West, the rodeo is a firm reminder that this is still cattle and sheep country. The town also caters to farmers and tourists.

You now turn straight north on U. S. 285 for four miles, then turn east on a well-graded county road to MOSCO (fly). A mile north of town the road turns east again across sage flats spotted with gleaming white alkali beds, then past SAN LUIS LAKE.

That is not a mirage you see before you — it is the GREAT SAND DUNES NATIONAL MONUMENT. Here nature has played a strange geological trick — a small Sahara desert bordering a fertile valley. Barren, mysterious, forbidding, endlessly fascinating, the dunes rise abruptly and surprisingly before you 800 and more feet above the valley floor like a giant's sandpile dumped at the base of MT. BLANCA. The road curves into the monument area where there are picnic grounds and water is available.

You learn that most geologists agree that the prevailing southwest winds lift the light sandy soil of the SAN LUIS VALLEY and blow it against the barrier of the SANGRE DE CRISTO MOUNTAINS, where the winds lose their force, causing them to drop the sands which in turn forms the dunes.

Flowing out of the mountains bewildered MEDANO CREEK ends up going nowhere. This mixed-up stream behaves like any stream headed for the sea, but it never gets there. Instead it abruptly disappears in the dunes. It is believed that INDIAN SPRINGS, a few miles away, is where the river reappears.

The dunes move constantly which means there is little vegetation except around the borders. Every year old wagon wheels, mule and horseshoes, and other objects are uncovered by the winds, showing where immigrants got lost and left their belongings behind. You are not allowed to drive into the dunes or hike into them very far as they are treacherous. You may climb a nearby dune and get a good look at these weird sand-piles which "sing" or "moan" as they shift and move about. If you happen to be here during a thunder storm, your hair will stand on end and crackle with static electricity. You'll enjoy walking barefoot in the sand, and some people bring their skis for sport.

When you leave the dunes, return to ALAMOSA on U. S. 160. Our By-Way tour goes east on this highway skirting the foot of MT. BLANCA which dominates this end of the valley. Snow-covered most of the year, the great peak is extremely impressive because it rises so abruptly from the valley floor without benefit of foothills. The Indians have always held it in great reverence.

BLANCA is a farming community founded in 1908 as a result of land drawings. FORT GARLAND is named for the nearby abandoned army fort, and is primarily a Spanish-American farming community. U. S. 160 continues north and east bisecting the huge TRINCHERA RANCH, which is a remnant of the mammoth Mexican SANGRE DE CRISTO LAND GRANT given in 1843. The highway now climbs up LA VETA PASS, then goes on to WALSENBURG, joining Interstate 25.

Our By-Way tour turns south from FORT GARLAND on State 159 to OLD FORT GARLAND a mile south of town, bordered by immense cottonwoods. The fort was built in 1858, a haven for immigrants who had traversed bleak, Indian-infested lands and now needed protection from the Ute Indians. Kit Carson spent much time here trying to keep peace between the white and red men.

The fort was abandoned in 1883. It was acquired by the State Historical Society of Colorado a few years ago and they have restored some of the buildings. There is an excellent museum with exhibits pertaining to the area. Be sure to notice some of the old santos (saints) made by the Spanish-Americans and discussed earlier.

South of the fort State 159 continues through irrigated farm-lands to SAN LUIS, seat of COSTILLA COUNTY, and one of the oldest settlements in COLORADO dating from 1853. Also a part of the Mexican Land Grant, the small town has many adobe houses and old buildings including the SALAZAR STORE which dates back to 1857 and is the oldest continually operated store in the state. The old stone CHURCH OF THE MOST PRECIOUS BLOOD (Roman Catholic) was erected in the 1860's. The oldest adobe house in town, built in 1852, is now covered with pink stucco.

Our By-Way tour turns west from SAN LUIS on State 142 through fertile farm lands bordering the RIO GRANDE RIVER which is cutting its southward path through the valley.

About two miles west of the Rio Grande River bridge a country road turns south less than a mile to the historic KING MINE, the oldest turquoise mine in COLORADO, and the deepest one in existence. First mined by prehistoric Indians, the old workings were discovered by Pervine King in 1890 while prospecting for gold. (Get permission to dig.)

You continue west on State 142 to MANASSA, another Mormon settlement, founded in 1878. The village is best known as the birthplace of the "Manassa Mauler," Jack Dempsey, World's Heavyweight Boxing Champion from 1919 to 1926.

State 142 then joins U. S. 285 where you turn north, returning to ALAMOSA.

◀ *The Great Sand Dunes*

Durango - Mesa Verde Area

By-Way Tour No. 5

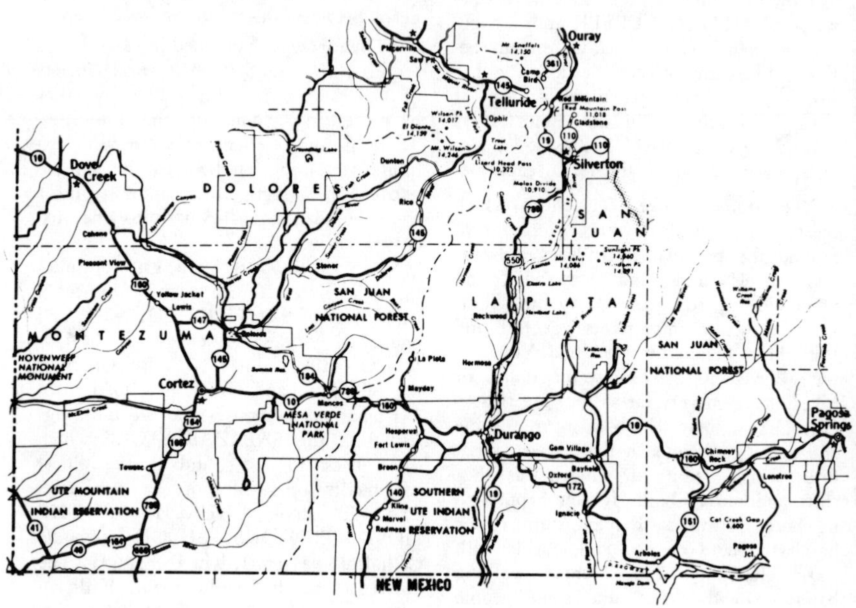

One of the most historic and romantic areas of the state is the "Four Corners" region where the states of COLORADO, New Mexico, Arizona and Utah share a common corner — only place in the U.S. where this happens. For thirteen centuries of prehistory this area fostered a more advanced culture than has been discovered at any other point north of the Azores. These people had an established culture before the Christian era.

Centuries later the Utes and the Navajos fought over parts of this country. Escalante came in 1776, seeking a route to the Spanish Missions in California.

But it wasn't until 1860 that a few men drifted in to seek gold. The discovery of gold and silver in the SAN JUANS, the LA PLATAS and the SAN MIGUELS brought the first white settlers. The building of the D&RG and the RIO GRANDE SOUTHERN narrow gauge railroads further developed the territory.

Today's economy is based on vast ranches, agriculture, some hard rock mining and tourists. Sparkling clear streams, endless jagged mountain peaks and meadows, forests of spruce, pine, fir and aspen, and jewel-like lakes lure the visitor for fishing, hunting, hiking, mountain climbing, rockhounding or just plain loafing.

But the biggest boom to the area has come through the development of vast oil and gas fields and the uranium mines south and west on the COLORADO PLATEAU.

Our By-Way tour starts at PAGOSA SPRINGS (healing water), largest warm mineral springs in the world, situated near the base of WOLF CREEK PASS. For many years the Utes and Navajos fought for the right of possession of these mineral springs.

An interesting off-the-beaten-path trip to DURANGO is taken by going south from PAGOSA SPRINGS. This road takes you through several picturesque Spanish-American villages a n d t h e SOUTHERN UTE RESERVATION. This is a three-culture land, indeed, and you will feel as though you are in another world. Indian culture blends with Spanish and to a small extent with American. The Ute Indians farm small tracts of land along the river banks and raise cattle and sheep on the dry sage-dotted hillsides.

Almost from the time you leave PAGOSA SPRINGS you are in the SOUTHERN UTE INDIAN RESERVA-TION until you join U.S. 160 near DURANGO. At PAGOSA JUNCTION the road swings west up and around an arm of NAVAJO DAM and RESERVOIR built in the 1960's to impound the waters of the SAN JUAN and LOS PINOS RIVERS.

Next you pick up State 151 and make a sharp left turn into ARBOLES. The highway then angles northwest into IGNACIO.

Here is the CONSOLIDATED UTE AGENCY HEADQUARTERS where the Federal Government maintains a school for the Ute and Navajo children, and a hospital. Two types of business flourish in IGNACIO — supplies for the Indian and Spanish-American farmers and ranchers, and a thriving business in handmade Indian articles. Navajos come to sell their exquisite silver and turquoise jewelry. The Utes make excellent leather work — moccasins, hat bands, purses and belts all heavily beaded — and they weave willow baskets. The famous Ute Chief Ouray and two other well-known chiefs, Ignacio and Buckskin Charley, are buried in a small cemetery across the LOS PINOS RIVER.

The SOUTHERN UTE TRIBE owns and operates a unique year-round Tourist Center featuring Indian decor. There is a 38-unit motel called PINO-NUCHE (PINE RIVER INDIANS) with a beautiful outdoor swimming pool, a restaurant, lounge, museum and an arts and crafts shop.

Leaving IGNACIO take State 172 northwest to U.S. 160 and on into DURANGO.

Our regular By-Way tour follows U.S. 160 from PAGOSA SPRINGS west about two miles. A gravel road goes northwest to WILLIAMS CAMPGROUND, entrance to the SAN JUAN PRIMITIVE AREA which lies at the western foot of the CONTINENTAL DIVIDE. Excellent for fishing and hunting.

The tour continues west on U.S. 160 to CHIMNEY ROCK. Once the home of the *Anasasi* — the "Ancient Ones" — CHIMNEY ROCK, a strange rock formation on a high mesa, is controlled by the U.S. Forest Service. Prehistoric Indian ruins dating back about 1,000 years have been excavated. There are many unexplored Indian mounds nearby. Legend has it that there is buried treasure here also. The area will be open to visitors as soon as provisions can be made to accommodate them as at MESA VERDE NATIONAL PARK.

BAYFIELD has become a rendezvous for rockhounds. Two miles west of town is GEM VILLAGE said to be the only rockhound community in the U.S. The population fluctuates with the season. Here you can buy, sell or trade for rock and mineral specimen from the immediate area as well as from many parts of the world.

From GEM VILLAGE you continue along U.S. 160 to a junction with U.S. 550. South on this highway in Farmington, New Mexico, with nearby AZTEC RUIN NATIONAL MONUMENT, similar to MESA VERDE NATIONAL PARK, but not as large. The great oil

The Utes once inhabited about half of Colorado

An old miner's shack is slowly giving way to nature

and gas development at Farmington has brought a real boom to the area.

Our By-Way tour turns north on U.S. 550. About two miles from the junction you pass CARBON MOUNTAIN on the left, an odd geological freak which insists on moving every so often and is nicknamed "walking mountain." Geologists do not agree as to what is making it misbehave.

Three miles beyond is DURANGO (watering place) founded in 1880 when the D&RG laid its tracks to this point. It's a picturesque little city lying in the shadows of the massive granite LA PLATA MOUNTAINS which form an imposing sawtooth barrier to the west.

If you are interested in the archeology of southwestern COLORADO the Public Library has an excellent collection of books on the subject. The SPANISH TRAILS FIESTA, held the first week in August, is a rousing western rodeo with one added attraction. The neighboring Ute, Navajo and other southwest Indians add their color to the fiesta with their native dress and pictorial dances.

The Vanadium Corporation of America's plant is the largest uranium processor in the world using radioactive ore hauled in from the COLORADO PLATEAU.

Every summer the eyes and feet of railroad buffs and other visitors turn to DURANGO, departure point for the excursion train on the only narrow gauge railroad left in America (see By-Ways Tour No. 2).

A spectacular drive east up RESERVOIR HILL takes you along a scenic drive overlooking DURANGO and the ANIMAS VALLEY. FT. LEWIS COLLEGE, moved here from south of HESPERUS, has an attractive campus. The college charter grants free tuition to the Ute, Navajo and Pueblo Indians and many of them take advantage of this privilege.

Just west of town is DURANGO SKI AREA. The rockhound will find many shops in DURANGO catering to his taste.

Our By-Way tour continues west on U. S. 160. The LA PLATA (silver) MOUNTAINS rear upward across the western horizon. Next is the small farm village of HESPERUS, an outfitting point for sportsmen and miners.

North from HESPERUS follow a well-graded road along the LA PLATA RIVER. The road climbs up a rugged canyon with the snow-capped LA PLATA peaks beckoning you. MAYDAY MINE and the nearby IDAHO MINE produced millions in gold early this century. They are still worked sporadically. There is a good rock cutters' and polishing industry at MAYDAY.

PARROT CITY, founded in 1874, was the first county seat until DURANGO was built. The COMSTOCK was the largest mine with both gold and silver being found. No old buildings remain at the townsite which is now the Parrot Ranch. Nearby the LUCKY MOON MINE has been worked recently.

A couple of miles beyond is LA PLATA with a few rakishly tilted buildings sagging on the meadow. The GOLD KING MILL is three miles farther. At one time a sagging suspension bridge connected the mill with the old boarding house. A foot trail leads to the GOLD KING and COLUMBUS MINES. The rockhound will find interesting ore specimen on the dumps.

Back on U. S. 160 our By-Way tour curves northwest nine miles climbing to sage-strewn high plateau country. Now U. S. 160 drops down into MONTE-ZUMA VALLEY which is a well-developed agricultural area. You'll see large, prosperous cattle ranches and fields of grain. MANCOS is a farming and ranching center catering to the tourist in the summer. Miners also outfit here.

A graveled road leads fishermen northeast to JACKSON GULCH RESERVOIR and other fine fishing lakes and streams in back country. Big game is plentiful too.

Our By-Way tour now twists across a broad plateau studded with gray and purple sage, bright green juniper and scrub cedar. At the junction of State 136 you turn left to MESA VERDE NATIONAL PARK.

It's like a trip to another age when you visit the centuries old ruins at Mesa Verde — pictured here is the Cliff Palace

Ruins at Hovenweep National Monument

The black-topped road starts climbing almost immediately winding up an escarpment called the "knife-edge." You twist and turn on a thrilling shelf road which offers you long vistas. When you reach the mesa top you are 2,000 feet above the MONTEZUMA VALLEY.

Now you turn away from the cliffs and strike out across the flat mesa, winding through a forest of pinon pine and scrub juniper interspersed with some ponderosa pine and fir. This tableland is 15 miles long and 8 miles wide covering an area just under 80 square miles at an elevation of 7,500 to 8,700 feet.

It is a land of mystery and enchantment, the air is highly invigorating, the days are warm, the nights cool, and the sunsets famous. This unique National Park is the only one dedicated to the study and preservation of the works of men. All the others are dedicated to grandeur and the wonders of nature.

Be sure to spend an interesting half hour in the museum where you will get a good background outlining the main features of the remarkable stone age civilization that flourished here over a thousand years ago. There are four main periods, each graphically outlined and explained. This understanding will add to your enjoyment of the park.

MESA VERDE became a park in 1906. The high spots to see are SPRUCE TREE HOUSE, FAR VIEW HOUSE, CLIFF PALACE, which housed about a thousand people, SQUARE TOWER HOUSE, which still has some of the original red and white clay plaster, LONG HOUSE, BALCONY HOUSE and the SUN TEMPLE. Conducted tours lead you directly to some of them; others may be viewed across the canyon where they give you an eerie feeling as if you were gazing into yesterday.

Our By-Way tour returns to U. S. 160 and turns west across a plateau, then descends to the DOLORES RIVER VALLEY and CORTEZ (named for the Spanish explorer). Founded in 1887 when the area was thrown open to ranchers, it is still a ranch and agricultural supply center. However, the uranium and oil discoveries on the COLORADO PLATEAU have boomed the town.

The buff sandstone business buildings contrast sharply with the sleek modern, neon-lighted architecture built recently. Ute and Navajo Indians, modern as today but clinging to many of their ancient customs, lend color to the streets.

Another side trip continues northwest on U. S. 160 across what was formerly sagebrush plateaus where for many years that desert plant grew shoulder high, and the land was used mostly for sheep and cattle grazing. Now great areas of sagebrush have been bulldozed out and the land planted to beans which grow like Jack's proverbial beanstalk in this arid land and give bumper crops wherever irrigation is available.

YELLOW JACKET is another farming community, named for the thousands of wasp nests which plaster the nearby canyon walls. Indian pictographs and dinosaur bones are found in the canyons. ACKMEN is also a supply center and an Indian trading post. A back country road goes west, then south from PLEASANT VIEW to HOVENWEEP NATIONAL MONUMENT on the COLORADO border.

DOVE CREEK is another agricultural center made prosperous by the bumper bean crops and more recently by the uranium and oil boom.

Our By-Way tour takes State 145 straight north out of CORTEZ to DOLORES, another ranch, lumber and tourist center. Here again you enter the SAN JUAN NATIONAL FOREST. Now you follow the DOLORES RIVER (shortened from the Spanish meaning "The River of Our Lady of Sorrows") to a land of lakelets, streams and ice-eaten mountains which curves northeast through wide alfalfa fields past MILLIGAN RESERVOIR to STONER. There's a popular ski center here.

Gold was discovered near RICO in 1866 but the Utes drove the miners out. The area boomed in 1878 with the discovery of gold. RICO was built in 1879, after rich deposits of lead carbonate of silver were found on NIGGER BABY HILL. RICO still has its share of false front buildings and retains much of its early charm. It was a riproaring gold camp with a later history of horse thieves. The ENTERPRISE, the PELICAN, the ELECTRIC LIGHT and the ATLANTIC CABLE were some of the big paying mines.

Leaving RICO our road follows the old ore-wagon road which crossed the river 40 times in 40 miles before bridges were built.

LIZARD HEAD PASS is at the crest of the SAN MIGUELS and is dominated by the fantastic peak which gives the pass its name. This peak is a treacherous pile of rotten rock and is shunned by most mountain climbers because it is dangerous. The roadbed of the old narrow gauge railroad, called "The Galloping Goose," may be seen to the right. At one time a huge wooden shed stood here covering the tracks to protect them from the heavy snow drifts which piled up 15 to 20 feet deep in the winter.

As you drop down off the pass magnificent azure TROUT LAKE comes into view surrounded by towering naked peaks. The sheer granite walls of SAN BERNARDO MOUNTAIN rising to a point is often compared with the Matterhorn in Switzerland.

The road continues to wind through forested hills. Ahead you will catch glimpses of the triangular-shaped granite OPHIR NEEDLES. Halfway down the mountain was the old OPHIR LOOP, a spectacular piece of railroad engineering. In order to eliminate excessive grades, the railroad track was laid in the shape of a large horseshoe partly supported on high wooden trestles. The hamlet here is called OPHIR where the railroad shipped ore. Two miles away is OLD OPHIR, once an important mining camp, clinging to the mountain sides and gradually disintegrating.

At a road junction, the right fork leads to TELLURIDE, about three miles away, which produced over $60,000,000 in gold. Named for the tellurous ores found in the district, the town was first called Columbia when founded in 1875.

TELLURIDE, rich in history, is beautifully situated against a background of rugged peaks. To add to its theatrical effect, a glistening waterfall, twice the height of Niagara, spills from the mountain at the end of the street. The town is still alive, a combination of nicely painted homes and stores and dilapidated buildings deteriorating into nothingness.

The SMUGGLER, the SHERIDAN, the MENDOTA, the UNION and the TOMBOY were the big name mines. Some are still worked from time to time, but now mostly for zinc, lead and copper with gold and silver as a by-product. The TOMBOY is reached via a hair-raising road which originally served as a trail over which burros carried ore across the SAN JUANS and down into SILVERTON for smelting.

You return to State 145 and swing northwest following the meandering SAN MIGUEL RIVER through low hills which were denuded of trees during the mining fever boom and are now covered with grey and purple sage. VANADIUM, SAW PIT and FALL CREEK, all former mining camps but now ghost towns, pinpoint the road which has entered a beautifully eroded red canyon.

PLACERVILLE was founded in 1877 when gold-bearing sands were discovered. Then it became the principal loading point for sheep and cattle while the "Galloping Goose" still ran and continues this role. You'll see many grassy meadows where sheep graze.

Our By-Way tour completes the circle by following State 145 northeast to RIDGWAY, then picking up U. S. 550 south via the MILLION DOLLAR HIGHWAY through OURAY and SILVERTON back to DURANGO.

PART 4

TABLE OF CONTENTS

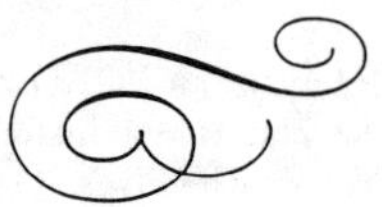

COLORADO

Just one jump back from the prairies and behind the front ranges of the Rockies is a chain of four rolling "parks" rimmed by snow-covered peaks and bisecting COLORADO from north to south. Buffaloes grazed for untold centuries on the lush wild hay in these parks. The Utes claimed them as their ancestral hunting grounds, but the Arapahoes, Cheyennes and other plains Indians came here to hunt too. The Utes also soaked their rheumatic joints and ailing bodies in every mineral spring from one end of the region to another.

This northwestern section of COLORADO, most of it on the fabulous WESTERN SLOPE, includes two of these parks — NORTH and MIDDLE PARK. The WESTERN SLOPE is rich in lore of many kinds — rich in legends of the Wild West, rich in the remains of its prehistoric occupants all the way back to the dinosaurs, rich in mining lore, rich in fertile farms and ranches, and rich in an unusual kind of scenery.

He who is seeking scenery flavored with history will find it in this region. It is a land of extremely rugged mountain terrain and level, fertile river valleys, dense woodland and fast-running streams, picturesque ghost towns and thriving modern cities.

Discovery of unbelievable gold and silver lodes lured miners by the thousands. Then came the ranchers and homesteaders to build a solid economy and help the region prosper. Today this area is a wonderland of ghost towns and working mining camps, prosperous ranches and fertile farms, and an all-season vacationland. Almost any trail leading from the main highways will take you into high country spots with more than one dream of a place to camp, fish, hunt or hike.

For the shutterbug there are ghost towns, aerial trams and unexcelled scenery. Sparkling streams and blue lakes lure the fly and spinner fisherman. The nimrod will find plenty of elk, deer and bear in season. Hiking, horseback riding, jeeping, camping and packing in are favorite vacation choices. Mountain climbers will find strings of "fourteeners" unparalleled elsewhere. The mountains and valleys are happy-hunting grounds for rockhounds and flower fanciers.

In fact, it's a country to linger in, to enjoy and to return to time after time.

Leadville and Golden Circle

By-Way Tour No. 1

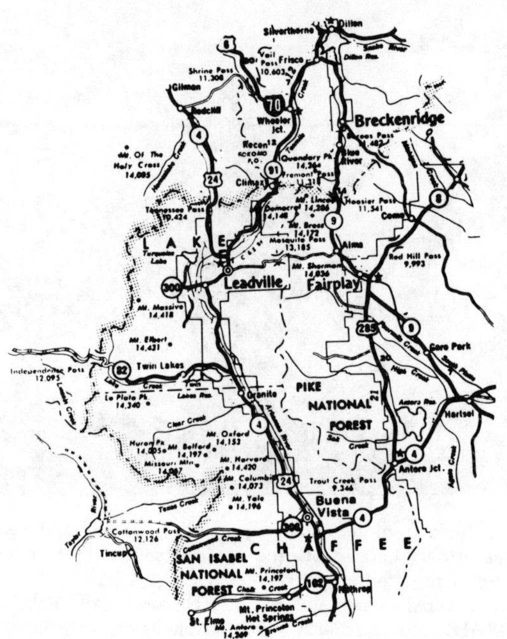

Don't let anyone tell you that mining is dead in Colorado. LEADVILLE, often called the "Cloud City" and most famous as a "Carbonate Camp," will belie this statement. Although the city has suffered a series of booms and busts since its founding in 1860, diversity of ores has made two-mile-high LEADVILLE, seat of LAKE COUNTY, one of the most tenacious of mining camps.

The LEADVILLE DISTRICT started in 1860 as ORO CITY (gold) in CALIFORNIA GULCH after Abe Lee, a discouraged miner and his party, dug through four feet of snow. Traces of gold were found and he shouted, "I've got Californy right here in my pan." Thus began one of the most famous of all mining camps. In the next ten years the gulch produced over $5,000,000 in gold, mostly from placer mining.

Later the town moved to its present site and was called LEADVILLE. By 1875 the placer gold was gone. Then A. B. Wood, a metallurgist, determined that the heavier reddish-yellow sand which had interfered with the "Big Toms" when sluicing for gold was actually almost pure carbonate of lead with a high content of silver.

This brought another boom and from it rose the Carbonate Kings and their massive fortunes: the Guggenheims, Samuel Newhouse, H. A. W. Tabor, Alva Adams, John Routt, and others. Additional great fortunes began here too: David May started the huge May Company chain in a tent in 1877. Charles Boettcher opened a hardware store, but invested in mining and from this he became a multimillionaire. The bubble burst in 1893 when silver was demonetized, and the fabulous silver era ended.

On the heels of this catastrophe came another boom when J. J. Brown discovered the LITTLE JONNY, a fabulous gold mine, in 1893. The boom was short-lived, so in the fall of 1895 a fantastic

ICE PALACE was built on CAPITOL HILL to stimulate trade and bring visitors. Constructed in castellated Norman style, the sparkling building contained ice statues, railroad exhibits, a skating rink, a dance hall, a dining room, a gaming room, curling alleys, other exhibits, and many carnival attractions. An unseasonably warm winter and early spring doomed the unique attraction to an early demise by March 1896.

Along fabled HARRISON AVENUE, the main street, are the ELKS OPERA HOUSE (once the Tabor Opera House); the HOTEL VENDOME, with its false-mansard roof, retaining much of its early charm in spite of some modern renovations and neon lights; the FEDERATED CHURCH, orginally the PRESBYTERIAN CHURCH, with its unusual roof line; the MAY COMPANY MONUMENT showing where David May built his first store; the SILVER DOLLAR GRILL which housed a series of notorious saloons. At the top of the street are the HEALY HOUSE and the DEXTER CABIN (moved from West 3rd Street), faithful restorations and owned by the COLORADO HISTORICAL SOCIETY. Here the stirring times are recorded in historic treasures, lovingly maintained. Their flower garden is delightful.

Scattered around town are the house with the ROOF-TOP EYE, 127 West 4th Street, built by the pioneer architect Eugene Robitaille; the huge red brick ROMAN CATHOLIC CHURCH OF THE ASSUMPTION with its steeple pointed to heaven (Baby Doe Tabor worshipped here); the charming wooden Gothic ST. GEORGE'S EPISCOPAL CHURCH; and of later vintage, ST. JOSEPH'S SLOVENIAN CATHOLIC CHURCH with its interesting murals painted by the local priest, Father Trunk. On East 5th Street is the TABOR HOUSE, home of the first Mrs. Tabor, who helped H. A. W. Tabor become the richest man in COLORADO. (Museum and fee.)

There are a number of interesting side trips. One of the most famous goes east on 7th Street up LITTLE STRAY HORSE GULCH to FRYER HILL where Tabor's MATCHLESS MINE paid off to the tune of over $10,000,000. The TABOR CABIN just south of the old shaft house (museum and fee) is where

Baby Doe Tabor, his second wife, lived for almost 36 years after Tabor told her on his deathbed, "Hold onto the Matchless." Baby Doe lived in abject poverty and froze to death in 1935. South of the MATCHLESS is the ROBERT E. LEE which was the richest producer in the district. Nearby is the LITTLE PITTSBURG which launched Tabor on his fantastic career after he grubstaked two miners with $17 worth of supplies.

This road offers a superb view of LEADVILLE squatting on a treeless plain (the early miners cut down all the trees to build shacks and get firewood). LEADVILLE'S dominant landmark is MT. MASSIVE in the SAWATCH RANGE. You can gaze across the ARKANSAS VALLEY to the RANGE and a 40-mile string of "fourteeners" (peaks over 14,000 feet) that hug the CONTINENTAL DIVIDE.

STRAY HORSE GULCH continues from East 5th street to the mines on CARBONATE HILL. The LITTLE JONNY MINE is here, discovered by J. J. Brown. His wife became known internationally as the "Unsinkable Molly Brown" after the *Titanic* disaster.

Up CALIFORNIA GULCH is the site of ORO CITY. Only gaping mine holes, yellow and gray dumps and sagging shaft houses testify to bonanza days. Here is where Horace and Augusta Tabor ran a store and post office before he "struck it rich."

The trip up EVANS GULCH takes you past another ghost town, STUMPTOWN, along the old stage road (now a trail crossing MOSQUITO PASS to ALMA and FAIRPLAY 22 miles away). Each summer a pack burro race is run over this trail from FAIRPLAY to LEADVILLE.

An improved road leads west on 6th Street to a junction. Take the road going to the north side of startling bluegreen TURQUOISE LAKE where there is good fishing. Northwest of here are the TURQUOISE CHIEF, the JOSIE MAY and two other mines which have produced profitably beautiful blue and green turquoise. (Rockhounds get permission to dig.)

The other road at the junction goes straight west, then curves up to the south side of TURQUOISE LAKE and swings on up to the entrance of the old

CARLETON TUNNEL.

The trail you have followed is part of the roadbed of the COLORADO MIDLAND RAILROAD which first climbed up over HAGERMAN PASS by what were known as the MIDLAND LOOPS, a series of long horseshoe curves. Then the railroad passed through 2200 foot HAGERMAN TUNNEL. Later the BUSK - IVANHOE TUNNEL (now CARLETON TUNNEL) was built in 1890 to eliminate the long pull over the pass.

Return past TURQUOISE LAKE, then take the road leading straight south past the State Fish Hatchery in MALTA, now a railroad station, but once the site of reduction mills and a prosperous charcoal-burning industry which flourished during the 1880's to furnish fuel to the LEADVILLE smelters. MALTA is at the lower end of CALIFORNIA GULCH. You now join U. S. 24 which takes you through STRINGTOWN, where smelter workers lived, to LEADVILLE.

As the highway curves north notice a huge black hill to the right formed from slag dumped here by the Harrison Reduction Works in the early days. You are now back on HARRISON AVENUE.

Our By-Way tour continues along the main street and follows U. S. 24 to a road junction. Here you take State 91 northeast which climbs rather quickly around wide curves leaving the ARKANSAS VALLEY.

Next is CLIMAX, a company-owned town where 90% of the world's molybdenum is mined. Here are the world's highest post office and supermarket. Built at the foot of BARTLETT MOUNTAIN, the mining operation is literally "moving the mountain" as you can see by the gigantic excavation to the right. Moly is used primarily to harden steel and in jet engines. By-products are tin, tungsten and pyrites for chemical acid.

You are now in the TENMILE MINING DISTRICT. As you leave CLIMAX great white silt dumps border the highway. To the left is a road up CHALK MOUNTAIN where the HIGH ALTITUDE OBSERVATORY, established in 1940 at 11,200 feet, is located to study solar rays. This is also a favorite ski area. Rockhounds will find good smoky quartz, sanidine feldspar, and clear topaz crystals.

You follow the highway a short distance to the top of FREMONT PASS (11,318 ft.) where at certain times of the year it is possible to see the MT. OF THE HOLY CROSS (Tour No. 3). Below you are more silt ponds which have covered ROBINSON, one-time gold camp and later a ghost town.

KOKOMO is off the road to the left about a mile. The tiny village is a semi-ghost town where the slender brick schoolhouse sitting forlornly on a lonely hill and the tiny Masonic Temple are both reminders of prosperous days. The town is now owned by the CLIMAX MOLYBDENUM CO., and is doomed eventually to be buried under the silt.

State 91 joins Interstate 70 and continues to FRISCO. Our By-Way follows the BLUE RIVER to BRECKENRIDGE over HOOSIER PASS (11,542 ft.), through the old gold camps of ALMA and FAIRPLAY (Vol. 1), then goes south on U. S. 285.

U. S. 285 is joined at ANTERO JUNCTION by U. S. 24 from COLORADO SPRINGS (Vol. 2). Now the highway climbs a low saddle, TROUT PASS (9346 ft.), entering SAN ISABEL NATIONAL FOREST. Before you is the wide ARKANSAS VALLEY with the SAWATCH RANGE thrusting its towering COLLEGIATE PEAKS—MTS. PRINCETON, YALE and HARVARD — into the COLORADO sky. Long canyons, U-shaped from glacial epochs, finger between them. The highway crosses the rushing ARKANSAS RIVER to a junction.

U. S. 285 turns south to SALIDA (Vol. 3). Rockhounds may want to take a side trip following U. S. 285 to some of the best spots for gem minerals in the country. DOROTHY HILL, SUGARLOAF MOUNTAIN and RUBY HILL are a rockhound's paradise. Smoky quartz, yellow topaz, red garnet and rounded pellets of black obsidian known as "black pearls" may be found.

South of NATHROP on U. S. 285 about three and one-half miles is a country road turning west. This leads to MT. ANTERO, named for a Ute chief. It's a tough hike or horseback ride to this region, but rockhounds may be rewarded with lovely blue aquamarines, rock crystal, smoky quartz and phenakite found in the pegmatite dikes.

State 162 leads west from NATHROP up GAS CREEK to MT. PRINCETON HOT SPRINGS, a famous spa for many years with a unique hotel which has, unfortunately, been torn down and moved to another state. HORTENSE, a ghost town, is directly north up the side of MT. PRINCETON. From the SPRINGS you follow the abandoned railroad grade of the DENVER, SOUTH PARK & PACIFIC ROAD west through striking CHALK CANYON whose stark whiteness is a challenge to shutterbugs at any time of the day. You sweep out over space around a rocky cliff, then climb up to ALPINE, another ghost town, perched far above the valley floor. Few buildings remain.

Now the canyon deepens and narrows with the chalky crags just overhead. As you round a curve, ST. ELMO, one of the earliest mining camps, is spread out below. A few people live here and there are more buildings than in most ghost towns. It was an important point for shipping over TINCUP PASS to the GUNNISON DISTRICT and ASPEN beyond. Later when the DSP&PRR built the ALPINE TUNNEL through the CONTINENTAL DIVIDE, ST. ELMO continued to prosper. The TRESSIE, the PIONEER and the IRON CHEST were the biggest mines and there are good ore specimen to be found in the old dumps.

Beyond ST. ELMO is ROMLEY with its MARY MURPHY MINE, and at HANCOCK, the FLORA BELLE, ALLIE BELL, and the STONEWALL were the big producers. A foot trail leads up to timberline to the east portal of the ALPINE TUNNEL which is now boarded up and unsafe for exploration. This tunnel was a real jinx. Built in 1881 at a cost of $200 a foot, the tunnel was the second highest in the world entering the mountain at 11,600 feet. Snowslides and coal gas caused many deaths. It was finally abandoned in 1910.

From the junction of U. S. 285 and 24 our By-Way tour turns north continuing on U. S. 24 past the Colorado State Reformatory to BUENA VISTA which was founded in the '70's by silver miners and enjoyed its share of the boom days.

Today the small town enjoys a leisurely pace. Head Lettuce Days in August pays tribute to that succulent vegetable which is raised in the fertile river bottoms and shipped nation-wide.

Take State 306 west from town along COTTONWOOD CREEK through the ghost town of HARVARD CITY founded in the '70's. The right hand road leads up toward old COTTONWOOD PASS which was an important route into ASPEN before INDEPENDENCE PASS to the north was built. The left hand road goes to COTTONWOOD LAKE with its excellent fishing. There's superb big game hunting throughout the whole area in the fall.

You continue north on State 24 past RIVERSIDE where the valley narrows and again enters the SAN ISABEL NATIONAL FOREST. CLEAR CREEK RESERVOIR to the left affords good fishing and boating.

The first gold in the region was found in 1859 at a place called KELLEY'S BAR, even before gold was discovered in CALIFORNIA GULCH near LEADVILLE. Two miles above KELLEY'S more gold was placered at GEORGIA BAR, where CLEAR CREEK empties into the ARKANSAS. A good dirt road to the left follows CLEAR CREEK to VICKSBURG and WINFIELD, founded in 1880. Some of the miners' cabins have been restored and the two ghost towns are now resort villages. Ore specimen may be found in the dumps.

Our By-Ways tour continues on U. S. 24 through GRANITE, founded in 1870, at the bottom of a ravine near the mouth of CACHE CREEK.

At a road junction State 82, a well-paved highway turns west past TWIN LAKES and over INDEPENDENCE PASS to LEADVILLE (Tour No. 3). Now you have a fine view of the "big two" — MT. ELBERT and MT. MASSIVE — dominating the upper ARKANSAS VALLEY. They are an everchanging picture of grandeur, strength and beauty. The arctic queen, MT. ELBERT (highest in COLORADO, 14,431 ft.), rises gracefully to a lofty cone and looks like a mountain ought to look.

MALTA is next at the head of the valley where the road swings east sharply through lower CALIFORNIA GULCH past STRINGTOWN and back to the "Cloud City" — LEADVILLE — most famous of all Carbonate Camps.

Rocky Mountain National Park Area

By-Way Tour No. 2

One of the best-known areas in COLORADO is ESTES PARK which has been a "must" in visitors' itineraries since the state became a tourist mecca. ESTES PARK is not a "park" in the truest sense — it is really a fabulous mountain playground and resort region catering to tourists with ESTES PARK VILLAGE as the hub. When ROCKY MOUNTAIN NATIONAL PARK was created in 1915 at its doorstep, ESTES PARK became doubly alluring.

Most of the ROCKY MOUNTAIN NATIONAL PARK'S charm lies in its infinite variety 405 square miles of some of the world's most spectacular scenery. More than 65 peaks over 10,000 feet and 42 over 12,000 feet with LONGS PEAK the granddaddy of them all, towering 14,255 feet above sea level. The park straddles the CONTINENTAL DIVIDE giving the visitor a real cross-section of mountain meadows and deep canyons, shaggy peaks and timberline vistas. Miles of wide, smoothly-paved, high gear, all-weather highways take you above timberline where you can experience Arctic circle terrain.

While ESTES PARK is the eastern gateway to the ROCKY MOUNTAIN NATIONAL PARK, the western entrance is on the other side of the DIVIDE at GRAND LAKE. World-famous TRAIL RIDGE ROAD (U. S. 34) connects the two resorts. In one day an ardent motorist can make a circle trip through ESTES PARK, with its granite mountains and dense forested slopes, ROCKY MOUNTAIN NATIONAL PARK, one of the few remaining unspoiled beauty spots in America, and picturesque, rustic GRAND LAKE (or reverse the direction) from DENVER, BOULDER, LONGMONT, LOVELAND and other eastern slope towns.

Our By-Way tour starts at GRANBY (U. S. 40) on the western slope located in MIDDLE PARK, one of the four flat mountain parks which interrupt the mountains running through the center of COLORADO from north to south. The small town is a farming, ranching, logging and tourist center.

You leave GRANBY going north on U. S. 34 following the COLORADO RIVER. GRANBY RESERVOIR and SHADOW MOUNTAIN LAKE were built to impound the waters of the COLORADO RIVER for irrigation in the summer and have 52 miles of scenic and recreational shoreline with all types of water sports.

GRAND LAKE VILLAGE, off the highway one mile on the banks of the lovely perpetually blue GRAND LAKE, is one of the nation's unique summer playgrounds. Nearby dude ranches dot the area. All types of recreation are available from the most strenuous sports to the most relaxing pastimes.

GRAND LAKE claims the highest yacht anchorage in the world with an annual regatta in August. Beautiful and palatial summer homes line the pine-fringed lakeshore. The lake, which is one source of the COLORADO RIVER, is a natural one dammed in a glacial moraine many centuries ago and believed to be bottomless. The dramatic view across the lake at Old Baldy is one you'll never forget. GRAND LAKE, almost surrounded by ROCKY MOUNTAIN NATIONAL PARK, is the west entrance to the park.

Our By-Way tour continues north on U. S. 34. As you start along the road it is hard to realize you are on a transcontinental highway, America's highest continuous automobile route, the unique TRAIL RIDGE ROAD. Most mountain highways utilize valleys and canyons to attain altitude. TRAIL RIDGE ROAD, one of the best engineered highways in the U.S., follows an old Ute Trail along the ridge tops and stays above timberline for eleven miles.

At this point the road parallels the North Fork of the COLORADO RIVER through a wide, sage-covered valley.

Now the highway climbs through dense lodgepole pine and spruce forests around a wide horseshoe curve with the river snaking far below. JACKSTRAW MOUNTAIN is a grim reminder of an 1872 forest fire. A few miles beyond is MILNER PASS where you cross the CONTINENTAL DIVIDE at 10,759 feet.

Greenish POUDRE LAKES, headwaters of the CACHE LA POUDRE RIVER, famous fishing stream, are just off the road. A trail leads to the left for about a mile to a crater on SPECIMEN MOUNTAIN where the rockhound will see pitch-stone (related to obsidian), some as soft as putty, blue and green agates, yellow opal and jasper, and geodes. A steep trail continues to the top of SPECIMEN MOUNTAIN, an extinct volcano. Sometimes mountain sheep are seen in the vicinity.

FALL RIVER PASS, 11,797 feet, has a stone shelter house and a museum which shows graphically the geological evolution of the park.

There's a never-to-be-forgotten view in every direction. To the west is the NEVER SUMMER RANGE, a craggy, bald spine with glaciers tucked in the

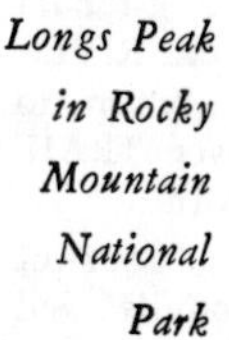

Longs Peak in Rocky Mountain National Park

canyons and often snow-covered the year around. The GORE RANGE to the southwest rises majestically. The MEDICINE BOW RANGE points a snowy finger north into Wyoming. The MUMMY RANGE to the north resembles a sleeping figure. To the east LONGS PEAK rears its snow-capped head in solitary majesty above the lesser peaks surrounding it.

Now you climb up to the highest point on the road, MONUMENT RIDGE, 12,185 feet, where a finder will point out the mountain peaks. Beyond, ICEBERG LAKE, a perpetual glacier, nestles below in a glacial cirque almost always frozen or with icecakes bobbing on the surface. Continuing along the highway, you see FOREST CANYON to the right cutting its deep gash. Across the canyon miniature sapphire-blue and emerald-green lakes are cupped gem-like on the high ridges. Herds of deer, elk and mountain sheep are seen from time to time far below on lush feeding grounds.

The private, unparalleled views from this road are literally "out of this world." High peaks and mountain ranges cut the sky in every direction. There are 42 peaks — count them — over 12,000 feet. You'll never forget those jagged mountains to the south with granite-capped LONGS PEAK putting a period at the end of the long chain. Flowing into the far eastern horizon are the high plains. Tortured trees, grotesquely twisted, mark the edge of timberline which you cross several times. Then the road dips down and is again bordered with forested hillsides to MANY PARKS CURVE.

You pass another forest burned in 1914, and go down past HIDDEN CREEK VALLEY where skiing has become very popular. Next is DEER RIDGE where you leave U. S. 34 and turn right, dropping down past beaver meadows to MORAINE PARK. This grassy valley is a wide-screen geological epic of rocks and debris which a prehistoric glacier pushed into the valley several thousand years ago. The MORAINE PARK MUSEUM is a "must" for those interested in the history of R O C K Y   M O U N T A I N   NATIONAL PARK.

An interesting side trip follows the BIG THOMPSON RIVER, southwest through TUXEDO PARK, then along MILL CREEK to HOLLOWELL PARK, another glacial moraine. Then comes blue-green BEAR LAKE, surrounded by high peaks, where a number of foot and horse trails lead through lovely primitive country.

Our By-Way tour follows the BIG THOMPSON RIVER down to ESTES PARK VILLAGE. Glaciers carved out the whole of ESTES PARK which accounts for some of its rugged beauty. It is scenically placed on a lovely mountain meadow surrounded by tall rugged peaks. The park offers the visitor almost any kind of vacation he desires.

A spectacular side trip follows U. S. 34 west along FALL RIVER to another park entrance. Beyond is HORSESHOE PARK, a wide alpine meadow.

FALL RIVER ROAD leaves U. S. 34 and follows the original route over FALL RIVER PASS before TRAIL RIDGE ROAD was built. This scenic, "old-time" mountain road is now one-way going "up only" and recommended only for expert drivers. A foot trail leads to YPSILON LAKE. Next in a glacial cirque is cobalt-blue LAWN LAKE. Very difficult trails lead beyond to CRYSTAL LAKE and TOWER GLACIER.

Now the highway crosses ROARING RIVER with HORSESHOE FALLS to the right, a favorite woodsy picnic spot. Then suddenly you start a steep ascent around hairpin curves through Englemann spruce and lodgepole pine. Across the way you can see picturesque HANGING VALLEY, believed to have been gouged out eons ago by a glacier. To the left FALL RIVER cascades down CHASM FALLS. Now the road twists through weird rock formations, past timberline where forest giants are reduced to pygmies, and finally across the rolling tundra to the rocky summit of FALL RIVER PASS. From here you may return to GRAND LAKE, or again over TRAIL RIDGE ROAD to ESTES PARK.

Three well-paved roads lead out of ESTES PARK for the foothills and plains. The first is perhaps the most popular and best-known — the spectacular BIG THOMPSON CANYON (U. S. 34) with its rugged grandeur which has cut its way through a rocky gulch with perpendicular pink granite cliffs dotted with spruce and pine. This highway continues through pictorial fruit country to LOVELAND.

The second road, State 66, follows the NORTH ST. VRAIN RIVER through a wide valley with occasional ranches. This was originally a toll road which connected LONGMONT and ESTES for 40 years. On the right are some of the quarries where pink or Lyons flagstone is removed. The stunning pink rock is used almost exclusively for the buildings of the UNIVERSITY OF COLORADO at BOULDER. The sandstone and shale formations offer pages of geological history for study. Rockhounds will find fossils.

LYONS is a small farming and tourist village at the gateway to the mountains where the two ST. VRAIN RIVERS join as they leave their canyons.

The third route goes south on State 7 past picturesque BALDPATE INN, then skirts the foothills of LONGS PEAK, covered with aspen groves and flower-studded alpine meadows.

Continue on the highway to COPE-LAND LAKE. This is the edge of the WILD BASIN AREA, a most rugged section of ROCKY MOUNTAIN NATIONAL PARK. An improved road goes west to COPELAND LAKE CAMP-GROUND, where marked foot trails will take you to OUZEL, BLUEBIRD, and THUNDER LAKE — all in very primitive country.

At ALLENSPARK is an old fireplace landmark which Alonzo Allen built as part of his cabin in 1864. Be sure to notice CHIEF'S HEAD MOUNTAIN which resembles an Indian's profile. Now the highway curves down wooded SOUTH ST. VRAIN VALLEY to RAY-MOND where State 160 goes straight south through WARD, NEDERLAND and CENTRAL CITY to U. S. 6.

Our By-Way turns south, staying on State 7 to BOULDER, home of the UNI-VERSITY OF COLORADO (See Vol. 1).

Now you pick up State 93 going south from BOULDER past ROCKY FLATS (AEC) to GOLDEN. You turn west and take U. S. 6, climbing up through CLEAR CREEK CANYON to the junction with I 70. Continue westward on I 70 past IDAHO SPRINGS and several villages to the junction where U. S. 40 leaves I 70. Our By-Way follows U. S. 40 to EMPIRE.

Founded by gold seekers in the early days, EMPIRE is now a popular year-round resort, catering especially to skiers in the winter. The highway enters ARAPAHOE NATIONAL FOREST and starts climbing rapidly. C R A T E R MOUNTAIN and ENGLEMANN PEAK are to the left.

At BERTHOUD PASS, 11,314 feet, you again cross the backbone of one of the roughest mountain ranges in the country, the CONTINENTAL DIVIDE. The pass was named for the engineer who surveyed it in 1861 for a railroad route which was never built. The famous mountain man, Jim Bridger, was his guide. Now BERTHOUD PASS is a popular ski area. A double chair lift operates the year around giving you unsurpassed sightseeing opportunities.

The road drops down rapidly from the pass via wide switchbacks with magnificent views of JAMES PEAK and others along the DIVIDE to the right. At the base of the pass is WINTER PARK, another ski resort, and part of the DEN-VER MOUNTAIN PARK SYSTEM (Vol. 1). Near WINTER PARK is the west portal of the MOFFAT TUNNEL where the D&RG RAILROAD emerges from a six-mile bore under nearby JAMES PEAK. This tunnel was the realization of a dream by David Moffat, early DENVER railroad builder.

To the right an improved road follows the old railroad bed up over CORONA PASS (abandoned by the railroad when the tunnel was built), then down through picturesque country to EAST PORTAL, ROLLINSVILLE, and BOULDER (See Vol. 1).

You are now following the FRAZER RIVER VALLEY which broadens as it approaches FRASER, vacation and ranching supply village. A good road takes off southwest up ST. LOUIS CREEK to BYERS PEAK CAMPGROUND. A trail leads on to ST. LOUIS LAKE and over ST. LOUIS PASS to the WILLIAMS FORK of the COLORADO RIVER. This is excellent fishing country.

TABERNASH, named for a Ute Indian Chief, is a railroad shipping center for stock and vegetables.

Once again our By-Way tour enters MIDDLE PARK and returns to GRAN-BY.

Glenwood Springs and Aspen

By-Way Tour No. 3

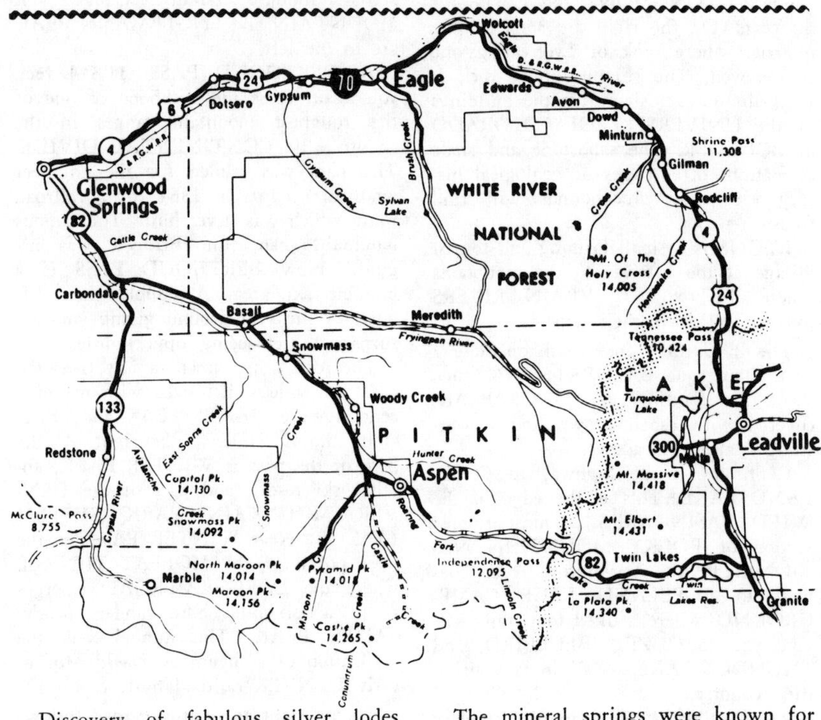

Discovery of fabulous silver lodes sparked the settlement of this area. Disappointed miners from the LEADVILLE and other mining districts with their "always-one-more-chance" attitude flocked to the ASPEN-GLENWOOD country, sure that this was their Eldorado.

Our By-Way tour starts in glamorous GLENWOOD SPRINGS, internationally-known spa for early COLORADO and Eastern Society, which began on a sandbar worth very little and developed into a fabulous resort worth plenty.

Founded in 1883 by Isaac Cooper because he believed in the healing properties of the mineral waters, the town has always been primarily a health and resort area. No discoveries of precious metals brought hordes of miners, but there are some coal mines in the vicinity. Instead, those who stopped here came to bathe their aching joints in the healing waters and to relax.

The mineral springs were known for centuries to the Utes who continued to come to them even after they were banished to a reservation in Utah. Chief Colorow, often dressed in a tall plug hat and frock coat slit up the back because of his size, strode the streets with haughty indifference.

Some of the Silver Kings of ASPEN discovered GLENWOOD SPRINGS and became interested in exploiting it as a health center. Heading a syndicate, Walter Devereux bought the springs site from Isaac Cooper, then had the COLORADO RIVER channel changed and the spa was launched.

A huge 42-room bathhouse and swimming pool were built in 1890 at a cost of $100,000 which still attracts thousands of visitors. This all year swimming pool, long as two football fields, is the largest hot mineral water pool in the world. Continually fed by mineral springs, frothy, boiling water gushes from one side and cold carbonated water flows in on the other side. In the winter a vapor barrier guards the swimmers and they can even swim in a snowstorm.

The palatial HOTEL COLORADO costing $850,000 was completed in 1893 and opened an era for international society. Copied after the Villa Medici in Rome, it is built of Roman brick and peachblow sandstone from the ruddy hills of the ROARING FORK VALLEY. Some renovation and modernization has been done, but the HOTEL retains much of its early charm.

Today GLENWOOD SPRINGS, cradled in its warm triangular valley surrounded by colorful mountains, continues the tradition of health and tourist resort. Giant cottonwoods planted by the early settlers form tall arches over the streets. Skiing is popular with RED MOUNTAIN chairlift just six blocks from the business district.

Our By-Way tour goes south on State 82 following the churning ROARING FORK RIVER.

About three miles south of town, LOOKOUT MOUNTAIN SCENIC DRIVE turns east through RED CANYON and SPRING VALLEY, then back via CATTLE CREEK, well-known fishing country.

Continue southeast along State 82 to the junction with State 133.

Turn right here a mile to CARBONDALE, founded in 1880, a prosperous ranching and farming community famous for its red soil potatoes and alfalfa crops. Dominating the town is symmetrical MT. SOPRIS, with its eternal mantle of snow and said to be the most photographed mountain in America.

Picturesque REDSTONE was founded in 1902 by John P. Osgood, head of the Colorado Fuel and Iron Co. Here he built the sandstone and frame 40-room INN of Dutch design with its well-known clock tower. The historic INN is now a swank resort, and much of its charm has been retained.

About a mile away he built himself a plush baronial 42-room frame and sandstone mansion of Norman design costing $2.5 million. Some of the walls were covered with hand-tooled elephant hide, silk brocade and gold leaf, and the wood-work is hand carved. Even the stable is paneled in walnut. It was furnished in rich Victorian and medieval style. Here Osgood established himself on a 4200-acre private hunting and fishing estate.

As the highway continues south, at times the road is reminiscent of New England country roads. Then the country becomes more rugged and the sentinels, turreted CAPITOL PEAK and straight-edged PYRAMID PEAK stand guard at either end of the jagged ELK MOUNTAINS sawing the sky — SNOWMASS MOUNTAIN, HAGERMAN PEAK, SNOWMASS PEAK and the MAROON BELLS. CHAIR MOUNTAIN to the south is upholstered in a fluffy white cushion of snow that never melts.

At PLACITA State 133 turns right continuing over McCLURE PASS to the GUNNISON COUNTRY and the GRAND MESA. You follow the other road which goes south to the ghost town of MARBLE huddling in a deep canyon with towering mountains on either side. Here the visitor sees a nostalgic leftover from the past standing white and vacant, the ghost town of MARBLE.

The first marble quarries were opened in 1890. The Colorado-Yule Company began operation in 1905.

The largest single piece of marble, a 100-ton block which took one year to remove, was quarried here and used for the Tomb of the Unknown Soldier in Arlington Cemetery. In addition, over 60 public buildings throughout the country have been built from marble quarried here.

With the coming of synthetic building material and marble veneers, marble prices declined. Snowslides, fires and floods harassed MARBLE. The disastrous cloudburst and flood of 1941 roared through the community wiping out practically all of the business and residential districts leaving a few battered frame buildings and some marble structures reminiscent of ancient Roman and Grecian ruins. You can walk about a mile up to the Yule Quarry to the east and pick up plenty of marble specimen.

Hiking, horse and jeep trails will take you into the back country setting of MAROON-SNOWMASS WILDERNESS AREA where deer and elk trails lead to shady pools filled with fighting trout. Don't forget your color camera. One trail continues along CRYSTAL CREEK to

Snowmass Lake at the foot of Hagerman Peak

the ghost town of CRYSTAL, then through scenic CRYSTAL CANYON over SCOFIELD PASS to the GUNNISON COUNTRY.

Our By-Way tour continues along State 82 from CARBONDALE to BASALT.

Another pictorial side trip follows the FRYING PAN RIVER straight east on a well-maintained road, formerly the roadbed of the COLORADO MIDLAND RAILROAD, past the handsome red SEVEN CASTLES with their medieval-like towers.

At NAST, a small summer resort, the road starts up through heavily forested slopes to HELLGATE, a breathtaking spot. Beyond in wilderness country are the headwaters of the FRYING PAN RIVER. According to one story, the river received its name because an early mining group lost most of their equipment fording the stream and had to use a frying pan to wash the sands for gold.

A dam and reservoir called the PAN-ARK has been built here impounding the waters of the FRYING PAN RIVER. This water is taken through a tunnel under the CONTINENTAL DIVIDE and empties into the ARKANSAS RIVER for irrigation on the eastern slope.

To the east the BIG TWO — MTS. MASSIVE and ELBERT — spraddle the CONTINENTAL DIVIDE. Near IVAN-HOE LAKE is the west portal of the now abandoned CARLETON TUNNEL (Tour No. 1).

Our By-Way tour continues southeast from BASALT along the railroad grade to SNOWMASS.

Here another road turns south bordered by lovely Englemann spruce taking you into more primitive back country. There are trails to SNOWMASS LAKE held in a brimming rock cup at the foot of snow-capped HAGERMAN PEAK. Here is a life-sized version of mountain scenery on wide-screen and in color.

From SNOWMASS follow State 82 almost to ASPEN.

One well-graded road turns southwest and takes you on one of the most beautiful side trips in the country.

Your first view of the MAROON BELLS is a dramatic one producing an impact on the eyes that can never be forgotten. The narrow canyon road widens into a green valley where fat cattle feed. There ahead of you the ruddy snow-tipped peaks pierce the blue sky, sometimes encircled with lazily rolling, fleecy clouds. Add to this stage-set aura MAROON LAKE whose green waters mirror the picturesque red mountains — three rock bell-shaped peaks with flaring sides seemingly welded together and incredibly beautiful. Not only are your eyes treated with color, but suddenly you realize that this scene is a challenge to any shutterbug. This is a place to sit and dream, to hike, and to fish.

The auto road ends here. CRATER LAKE is a one-mile hike above MAROON LAKE. Foot and horse trails lead to the MAROON-SNOWMASS WILD AREA for rugged pack trips.

Back on State 82, another dirt road turns southeast along CASTLE CREEK to the ghost town of ASHCROFT. Yapping Alaskan huskies are raised here for sled trips during the winter. H. A. W. Tabor (Tour No. 1) owned the nearby MONTEZUMA MINE. A foot, horse and jeep trail continues over TAYLOR PASS to PIE PLANT, TAYLOR RESERVOIR and TINCUP. (Vol. 3).

Our By-Way tour continues on State 82 to world-famous ASPEN, seat of PITKIN COUNTY, which has boomed twice — first with the discovery of silver and again with the discovery of powder snow. Founded in 1880 through the sweat and muck of mining, ASPEN today is an internationally-known ski center in the winter — home of the silky powder snow and breathtaking terrain whose precipitous slopes are a skier's dream. In addition, it is a cultural Mecca and popular vacation center in the summer.

Miners came from LEADVILLE in the '80's and gophered in the seven mountain peaks which ring ASPEN. Fabulous silver strikes resulted where thick matted wire silver and pure silver nuggets, like something out of the Arabian Nights, were found. Over $120,000,000 were dug out of the mines here in 20 years. The big producers were the ASPEN, the MOLLY GIBSON, the MIDNIGHT, the MONTEZUMA, the DURANT and the SMUGGLER — the latter producing the largest silver nugget ever mined, weighing over a ton and assaying 98% pure silver.

The silver panic of 1893 sealed ASPEN'S doom as a mining camp, although some mines are still worked, mostly for lead and zinc. For the next half-century the drowsy little town settled into a dreamy decadence. In the late '30's some ski enthusiasts started going to ASPEN, and ROCK RUN, a four-mile course considered by experts to be one of the most difficult in the world, was built. The MIDNIGHT MINE is only a couple of hundred feet east of the top of the RUN.

Today, the world's longest chairlift, which can carry 5,500 people per hour, unwinds up ASPEN HIGHLANDS. Here is an unexcelled panoramic view of the top of the nation — soaring mountain peaks, deep valleys, rushing rivers and forested hillsides.

ASPEN, however, is a round-the-calendar vacation spot. In the summer the mountain-girt village has swapped silver ore for the rich ore of culture. Today, ideas are important in the town as exemplified by the ASPEN INSTITUTE FOR HUMANISTIC STUDIES. Sparked and underwritten by Walter Paepcke, a Chicago financier, the INSTITUTE is dedicated to man's yen to listen, to talk and to learn. The ASPEN MUSIC FESTIVAL adds its stimulating contribution, and throughout the summer the unique tent-like amphitheater in the ASPEN MEADOWS resounds with music, lectures and discussions. ASPEN HEALTH CENTER is for the "tired businessman."

ASPEN has touched up its gingerbread facade. Nowhere is the past more faithfully preserved, painstakingly restored and enthusiastically retold. The historic HOTEL JEROME, the best known landmark, was built in the early 1900's at a cost of $120,000 and was a plush hotel in ASPEN's salad days. Today the HOTEL is a happy blend of western hospitality, Victorian charm and modern convenience.

Happily many of the old buildings have been preserved and renovated including the PITKIN COUNTY COURT HOUSE, the COMMUNITY CHURCH (formerly Presbyterian), and the WHEELER OPERA HOUSE which once was gutted by fire. The dingy old city hall, jail and firehouse have been transformed into delightful lodgings. Newer lodges have taken on Swiss architecture which seems to feel quite at home in these lofty Alps-like mountains, giving a spectacular, yet tasteful, blending of two periods.

Some of the original houses whose faces have been lifted include the GIBSON GIRL HOUSE, the WEBSTER HOUSE, the WAITE HOUSE and the VAN HOVENBERG HOUSE. The GHOST HOUSE, built by Henry B. Gillespie, one of the founders of ASPEN, is a "must."

Our By-Way tour leaves ASPEN on State 82 continuing along the noisy ROARING FORK to the GROTTOS and the DEVIL'S PUNCH BOWL near GROTTO CAMP GROUND. A short hike will show you where the turbulent river has hollowed out a series of fantastic bowls from solid rock.

Soon the highway starts up winding switchbacks, past the ghost town of INDEPENDENCE, with its weathered, forbidding structures clinging, precariously to the mountainside.

Barren, bleak INDEPENDENCE PASS (12,965 ft. and closed during the winter) is the highest auto pass in the state topping the CONTINENTAL DIVIDE. Even at this lofty height, mountain peaks tower on either side and unforgetable scenic vistas are spread before you. Now you drop down via long horseshoe curves into the LAKE CREEK VALLEY with breathtaking views of the SAWATCH RANGE on either side and the MOSQUITO RANGE to the east.

TWIN LAKES is one of the oldest summer resorts in COLORADO, founded soon after LEADVILLE. The GORDON, LITTLE JOSIE and TIGER MINES were worked nearby. The two beautiful lakes are fed by water from the ROARING FORK RIVER west of the DIVIDE which flows through a tunnel bored under INDEPENDENCE PASS. Summer cottages dot the lakeshore.

State 82 ends at U. S. 24 where you turn north through MALTA and LEADVILLE (Tour No. 1), then continue through rolling forested country along easy grades to TENNESSEE PASS (10,425 ft.) on the CONTINENTAL DIVIDE.

Now the highway drops down along the EAGLE RIVER past old brick kilns where charcoal was made for the LEADVILLE smelters. PANDO (ponds) was once a small sawmill center. During World War II the army built CAMP HALE here and trained ski troops. When the camp was abandoned, PANDO settled back to its quiet life.

North of PANDO you get the best view of MT. OF THE HOLY CROSS in the spring and early summer. A dirt road takes off to the left to the ghost town of GOLD PARK and a trail leading to old HOLY CROSS CITY.

Next is REDCLIFF, once a famous gold mine camp, where pure gold nuggets were taken from the GROUND HOG MINE. The HORN SILVER MINE, now just a few yellow dumps on the mountain side, once produced silver assaying 2000 ounces to the ton. Today lead, zinc and silver are still mined. The

weather-beaten houses are reached by long wooden staircases from the highway. A side road angles northeast over SHRINE PASS to I 70 through rugged back country.

Now the highway climbs a long winding road around a shoulder of BATTLE MOUNTAIN.

GILMAN was founded in 1886 by gold seekers who swarmed over the jagged cliffs, and the Leadville limestone outcroppings are pockmarked with their mines. The town, which clings precariously to the steep mountainside, is built out on a steep rocky promontory that rises several hundred feet above the thrashing EAGLE RIVER.

Just before reaching MINTURN, a dirt road turns straight south to TIGIWON, and beyond it are eight rough miles to where you can hike to the MT. OF THE HOLY CROSS.

MINTURN is another mining, railroad and lumber center with a zinc mill. Two miles beyond U. S. 24 joins I 70 and curves north, then west still following the EAGLE RIVER through WOLCOTT, EAGLE, and DOTSERO (Tour No. 4). Here the EAGLE empties into the COLORADO RIVER.

Now the highway swings southwest entering the 15-mile breathtaking, scenic GLENWOOD CANYON.

This river, using gravel and sand as tools, has been carving the stunning varicolored canyon for millions of years. The canyon is just wide enough for the broad highway on one side of the river and the D&RGRR on the other. Vistadomed diesel trains snake their way along the river passing through several small and smoke-blackened tunnels. A unique monument stands on the river bank with a miniature vistadome railroad car marking the spot where an official of the railroad dreamed up this unique car so that railroad travelers could truly enjoy such striking scenery.

HANGING LAKE PARK marks the beginning of a one-mile foot trail up to exquisitely blue HANGING LAKE, cupped on a sheer cliff and fed by the sparkling BRIDAL VEIL FALLS above. Plant life is petrified in the lake because of the water's mineral content.

Our By-Way tour continues through GLENWOOD CANYON another ten miles to GLENWOOD SPRINGS.

Steamboat Springs-Green Mtn. Dam Circle

By-Way Tour No. 4

A truly off-the-beaten-path trip is followed on this By-Way tour since it uses only a small part of two U. S. highways and the rest of the time follows state highways and county roads, penetrating deep into back country and wilderness area.

Due to its rugged terrain and inaccessibility much of this northwestern Colorado region was not settled until the 70's and 80's. Even today, the density of population in comparison to the rest of the state is small.

Gold was discovered in the HAHNS PEAK area in 1862 where the first settlements were made. But much of the country didn't open up until

STEAMBOAT SPRINGS, now the seat of ROUTT COUNTY, was founded in 1875 by James H. Crawford, a homesteader. The town was named for the peculiar "chug-chug" one of the springs made which sounded like a steamboat. When the MOFFAT RAILROAD was built, blasting destroyed the sound.

There are more than 150 active mineral springs in the immediate area including SODA, SULPHUR, IRON SPRINGS and the LITHIA SPRINGS, one of the few in the world, all located at the western edge of town. The Indians knew the springs well and made use of their medical properties. Popular today are the swimming pools and bath houses amply supplied by the natural springs.

A year around vacation center, STEAMBOAT SPRINGS has a variety of amusements for the visitor. Throughout the summer more than 400 miles of fishing streams and over 50 lakes lure the nimrod. There are scenic picnic and camping spots with numerous dude ranches offering pack trips. Many of the trails follow old Indian trails which Forest Rangers have cleaned up. Rockhounding for minerals and taking pictures add to the enjoyment. Two summer events are the Fourth of July Rodeo and the Square Dance Festival held the second Saturday in August.

STEAMBOAT SPRINGS has an international reputation with its skiing facilities and WINTER CARNIVAL held the second week in February. The town is perhaps one of the most ski conscious communities in the U. S. Children at the age of six get ski instruction. The high school band is mounted on skis for parading. The whole town backs WINTER CARNIVAL — a gala affair. World-famous HOWELSEN HILL is the center of the main event where in 1951 the American jumping distance of 316 feet was reached. In addition, slalom, cross-country and downhill skiing are performed in the perfect powder snow.

Skijoring — riding on skis behind fleet range ponies — is also enjoyed. Hurdle races, and ring and spear races add to the excitement. Snow and ice statuary — elk, snowmen, igloos, polar bears and penguins — dress up the street. One of the most exciting scenes during the carnival is to see the skiers at night, against a theatrical backdrop of dark mountains and a full moon overhead, zooming down the slopes brandishing flares and fireworks along the way.

A favorite picnic spot is about three and one-half miles east of town, where 200 feet of glistening water spills down FISH CREEK FALLS. For another short trip take State 36 north on 7th Street through STRAWBERRY PARK, named for the luscious fruit raised here.

Seven miles north is HOT SPRINGS, where you can boil your eggs for lunch in the bubbling water, and then picnic in a delightful woodsy area. Scenic BLACKMER DRIVE is a two-mile ride overlooking the town. Go south from Lincoln Avenue past the depot, cross the YAMPA RIVER and follow a marked trail.

ELK RIVER VALLEY is reached by following U. S. 40 west for two miles, then turning north on State 129. Prosperous working and dude ranches dot the valley which is barricaded by the

Beautiful
Fish Creek
Falls
at
Steamboat
Springs

PARK RANGE of the CONTINENTAL DIVIDE and the ELKHEAD MOUNTAINS to the west. CLARK, a tiny community, now caters to ranchers and tourists, but nearby hillsides show where gold, silver and copper have been mined, with the old ore dumps yielding good specimen.

For those who yearn for solitude and an outing of real "roughing it" there are many wilderness and wild areas in this region. These areas are usually accessible only by trail or water, free of nearly all artificial influence, and almost completely undeveloped. For such a trip turn east at CLARK along State 311 continuing along the ELK RIVER past BOX CANYON and SEED HOUSE to the MT. ZIRKEL PRIMITIVE AREA in ROUTT NATIONAL FOREST. The rugged SAWTOOTH MOUNTAINS of the PARK RANGE to the east stab the blue sky. A delightful pack trail turns southeast out of SEED HOUSE skirting the PARK RANGE. Over 20 fishable lakes are accessible along this route which eventually ends at U. S. 40 near RABBIT EARS PASS.

Gold was discovered in 1864 near historic HAHNS PEAK VILLAGE, a semi-ghost town at the base of the pictorial mountain of the same name. "Grass roots" or placer mining flourished for a time. Later hydraulic mining left behind the ugly gravel mounds. The village is now a small ranching and vacation center.

Now State 129 enters ROUTT NATIONAL FOREST. Beyond is COLUMBINE, another ghost town turned into a resort. At the ROYAL FLUSH MINE off the road two miles east on HAHNS PEAK there are still a few houses tumbling to ruin. Rockhounds will want to search the dumps for specimen.

Our By-Way tour leaves STEAMBOAT SPRINGS on U. S. 40 going south for four miles, then turns right on State 131. The road winds through lush hay meadows, grain fields and truck gardens in the verdant YAMPA VALLEY. Soon the highway enters a canyon with HAYBRO, ROUTT, OAK HILLS and OAK CREEK, all coal mining communities. High grade bituminous coal underlies the whole region from here to STEAMBOAT SPRINGS and west to MT. HARRIS and HAYDEN.

A good graveled road follows the old wagon trail northwest to PINNACLE and HAYDEN. This is good fishing, camping and hunting country. Picturesque granite cliffs close in as you near PHIPPSBURG, where the highway picks up the upper YAMPA RIVER. Another country road turns southwest to OAK CREEK CAMP GROUND in ROUTT NATIONAL FOREST, also known for excellent fishing and hunting.

YAMPA, named for the edible root of a plant which the Indians and early settlers ate, is a small western town lying on the rich bottom lands between the BEAR and YAMPA RIVERS. Irrigation makes possible some of the finest mountain lettuce grown anywhere. A well-graveled road leads southwest along BEAR RIVER to BEAR RIVER CAMP GROUND, another primitive fishing and hunting region also in ROUTT NA-

TIONAL FOREST.

Now State 131 swings southeast past rugged grey FINGER ROCK, a hard rock volcanic plug and long a landmark. Indian legend says a chief shook his finger defiantly at Manitou (God) and the chief's finger was turned to stone. TOPONAS named for nearby TOPONAS ROCK which the Utes thought resembled a sleeping lion, is at the junction of State 84.

This picturesque route turns east past TOPONAS ROCK through another part of ROUTT NATIONAL FOREST, then climbs GORE PASS (9524 feet). Alpine meadows filled with gorgeous stands of blue columbines, little pink elephants and deep blue leather flowers (clematis) put on a stunning show during the summer. The highway drops down across sage-brush hills to U. S. 40, where it's just six miles to KREMMLING.

Our By-Way tour continues southeast through EGERIA PARK. To the west is the WHITE RIVER PLATEAU with its many "Flat Tops," extinct volcanoes.

A real off-the-beaten-path and extremely scenic route turns west on a well-graveled road going southwest parallel-ing both the railroad and the COLO-RADO RIVER. Fossils of prehistoric animals and fish may be found in the canyon walls. The GREAT PAGODAS (also called circular BEEHIVES), like gigantic red Buddhist temples, line the river for five miles, their huge red scallops banded with green and grey stone, and studded with pines. The rush-ing river dashes along in white foam and crystal clarity.

Below BURNS the canyons are like huge slices of eroded clay stratas with gypsum sandwiched between. At BUSS PLACE, a well-graded road turns north-west into the primitive country around SWEETWATER LAKE, where there is superb fishing and hunting. The beauti-ful pink coloring and erosion of the canyons along SWEETWATER CREEK strongly resemble Bryce Canyon National Park in Utah.

Return to the main road and drive another five miles. Again there is a well-graded road leading northwest past COF-FEE POT SPRING to DEEP LAKE in the midst of several blue-water lakes. This is breathtakingly beautiful country and you may want to take the road just

for the view. MT. SOPRIS rises to the south in majestic beauty. The FLAT TOPS stretch to the north. The moun-tains walling in the COLORADO RIVER VALLEY to the east and south are a prism of color—pink, red, orange, green, gray and brown. CARBONATE, a real ghost town and the first seat of GAR-FIELD COUNTY, is almost inaccessible except by hiking or on horseback along a rugged six-mile trail which wanders in and out, finally going up on the FLAT TOPS to 11,00 feet above sea level. A few sagging buildings remain in this once prosperous silver and lead camp. Ore specimen may be found.

Again you will return to the main road. To the right is an extinct volcano marked by its dark lava flow. Two miles beyond is DOTSERO on Interstate 70, where the mighty COLORADO RIVER is joined by the EAGLE RIVER. Here the D&RGRR, which you have been following, joins the Royal Gorge Route from PUEBLO. From this point a survey of the COLORADO RIVER was made in 1885. At the initial point on the record it reads .0 (dot zero), hence the name, DOTSERO.

You turn east on I 70 and U. S. 24 crossing some of the high plateau country of COLORADO, where only sage and mesquite grow except where irrigation is available. White limestone cliffs south of the EAGLE RIVER identify GYP-SUM, a farming and mining community where gypsum is quarried for use as insulating material. Now the highway enters a broad, ranch-dotted valley to EAGLE.

A well-graded road turns southeast from the town along BRUSH CREEK to the ghost town of FULFORD, where many of the cabins and buildings still stand. Founded in 1890 as a gold camp, FULFORD also enjoyed a silver boom in 1912. Treasure hunters are still looking for a lost gold mine for which there are accurate directions, but no one has ever found it. Along this road you'll get marvelous views of the MOUNT OF THE HOLY CROSS (By-Way Tour No. 3) and the primitive WOODS LAKE fishing country.

Continuing on I 70 and U. S. 24 you climb into mountainous country again through a narrow canyon of highly col-ored red sandstone. A few miles beyond is WOLCOTT. The small town was once an important supply point for ranches to the north before the MOFFAT RAILROAD was built. Continuing east on Interstate I 70 follow the sparkling EAGLE RIVER where the fishing is usually excellent.

RED AND WHITE MOUNTAIN dominates AVON, a tiny farming community. Then U. S. 24 leaves I 70 at a junction and continues south to LEADVILLE (Tour No. 3). You stay on I 70 passing VAIL VILLAGE. This ski community started from scratch in the late 1950's and continues growing. Contemporary and Swiss architecture combine to make this a most attractive area. Ski slopes unsurpassed anywhere bring visitors from all over the world. The gondolas run year-round from which visitors get magnificent views of many COLORADO peaks.

The highway continues up and across scenic VAIL PASS which in the fall turns into a flaming spectacle. At the junction with State 91, our By-Way turns north along TEN-MILE CREEK to FRISCO. Now a resort and fishing center, FRISCO was a gold camp founded in the 1870's.

The highway now crosses DILLON DAM and our By-Way turns left on State 9 following the sparkling BLUE RIVER.

GREEN MOUNTAIN DAM and LAKE are noted for rainbow and brown trout with Kokanee Salmon now introduced. All types of water sports are available and cabins dot the lakeshore.

KREMMLING on U. S. 40 is a ranching, lumber and tourist center. Millions of feet of lumber are shipped each year which is sawed and cured into the well-known knotty pine. A scenic drive up the cliffs north of the town will give you wide views of the valley. Many Indian arrows and fossils of ancient creatures are found here. Real Western barbecues are held during the summer with a Wild Game Barbecue in the fall which attracts many people.

For a real off-the-beaten-path trip drive two miles south of KREMMLING on State 9, then turn southwest on State 11, a well-graveled road. To your right the D&RG parallels the COLORADO RIVER as they enter a narrow rocky slash in the mountain formerly called "The Trough." The railroad and river go through one of the deepest and most rugged of all western gorges — spectacular GORE CANYON — which was gouged out by the river and separates the PARK and GORE RANGES. The river churns and boils as it sweeps through the gorge. The highway follows the old shelf trail which was blasted out of solid rock to haul supplies when the railroad was built in 1906. At times you are 2000 feet above the canyon floor, where you can gaze down on the river and the railroad. Other times you get down close and follow them. You'll see CATHEDRAL ROCKS, familiar landmarks. The shutterbugs will find a real challenge to photograph the foaming river lashing and racing between the colorful canyon walls. State 11 ends at STATE BRIDGE.

Our By-Way tour continues north from KREMMLING on U. S. 40 through the sage-covered MUDDY CREEK VALLEY. MUDDY PASS (8772), lowest saddle on the CONTINENTAL DIVIDE, is at the junction with State 14, going north to WALDEN (Tour No. 6). U. S. 40 curves west and crosses RABBIT EARS PASS (9680 feet), also on the CONTINENTAL DIVIDE, and named for the twin upthrusts of sharp rock on the mountain peak to the north.

This is one of the most beautifully wooded passes in COLORADO. Pine trees dominate, but there are large stands of quaking aspen, bright green mountain ash with striking red and orange berries in late summer, scrub oak, and dwarf willows. The forest floor is thickly carpeted with giant ferns and the blue columbines grow to an astounding size. Autumn is a thrilling colorama dominated by crimson and gold that flames among the evergreens.

Now the highway starts its long, winding descent back to the YAMPA RIVER VALLEY, where you will be treated to one of the most arresting panoramic views in COLORADO. Below, the valley is spread out like a great green and yellow relief map threaded by the YAMPA RIVER which twists and turns like a giant silver snake. A blue haze caresses the distant peaks and valleys. Our By-Way tour ends at STEAMBOAT SPRINGS.

Grand Mesa

By-Way Tour No. 5

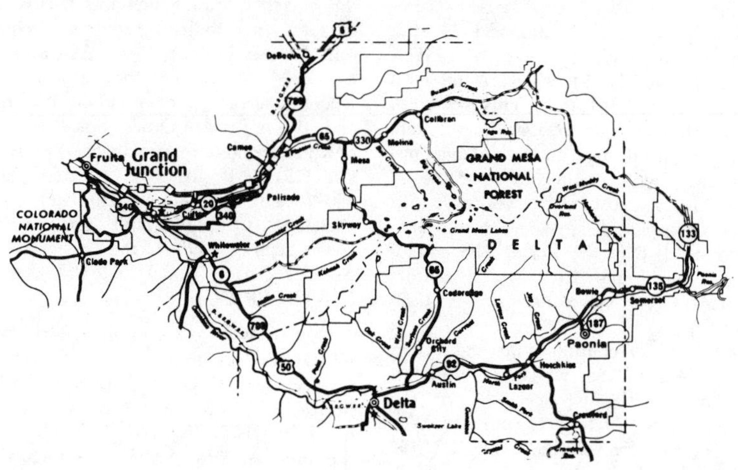

The 18th Century Spanish explorers who toiled through this country aptly named the huge flat-topped mountain "GRAND MESA" (large tableland). They were amazed, as is every succeeding generation, to find a great area of some 53 square miles holding in its lap over 200 sparkling lakes.

It is a country to delight the fisherman and hunter — elk, deer, and bear abound. The lakes are filled with gamey trout — rocky mountain, German browns and cutthroat. Great evergreen forests provide every type of camping area with trails for hikers and horseback riders.

GRAND JUNCTION, founded in 1881 after the Utes were removed to their reservation in Utah, is the largest city in COLORADO west of the CONTINENTAL DIVIDE. For many years it was known primarily as a fruit shipping center — peaches, apples, apricots, pears, cherries, grapes and plums flourish in irrigated orchards.

The discovery of vast uranium deposits on the COLORADO PLATEAU to the west exploded a boom here after World War II. The boom has now leveled off, but modern GRAND JUNCTION is still growing. The development of the gilsonite, oil and gas fields to the north, and the various uranium plants in the vicinity all contribute to the city's economy.

A "must" side trip from GRAND JUNCTION is to COLORADO NATIONAL MONUMENT, 18,000 acres of weirdly eroded red sandstone highlands, cut by sheer-walled canyons. Many-layered ramparts, fluted columns and gigantic monoliths add their fantastic vivid beauty.

Our By-Way tour leaves GRAND JUNCTION on State 340 which will take you on a circle trip through the DINOSAUR BEDS near the COLORADO RIVER.

Here the rockhound may find pink snail shells and gastroliths (gizzard stones from dinosaurs' stomachs) and other prehistoric fossils. You turn across on State 340 swinging southwest across the DINOSAUR BEDS through colorful NO THOROUGHFARE CANYON, its exposed rocks sparkling with mica, feldspar and quartz. To the left is DEVIL'S KITCHEN. As you climb, the hillsides are pinpointed with juniper, pinon pine and mountain mahogany.

At COLD SHIVERS POINT is a panoramic view of the GRAND VALLEY to the east with its patchwork quilt of fields and orchards.

Now you are on the 23-mile RIM ROCK DRIVE which skirts the steep cliffs of RED, UTE and MONUMENT CANYONS. Hikers may want to take some of the marked trails down into the canyons. Overlooks are provided where you can catch glimpses of such stunning sights as CLEOPATRA'S COUCH, COKE OVENS, MONOLITH PARADE, WINDOW ROCK and other flaming monoliths.

Rockhounds will find this area a happy hunting ground. You cannot collect in the monument itself but at GLADE PARK, southwest of the MONUMENT on a dirt road and OPAL HILL northwest (near FRUITA golf course) opalized wood is found. At PINON MESA beyond GLADE PARK petrified wood, agate, jasper and chalcedony are found.

The road descends into FRUITA CANYON through a couple of tunnels, crosses the river and the D&RG tracks, then joins U. S. 6 and 50. You turn southeast and return to GRAND JUNCTION.

Our By-Way tour follows another route taking U. S. 50 past WHITEWATER to DELTA, the gateway to a fruit basket land.

Four miles east of DELTA, take State 65 (called the SKYWAY DRIVE) north through CORY, ORCHARD CITY and ECKERT to CEDAREDGE.

A few miles beyond is a unique museum reached through an old mine shaft with an interesting, though small exhibit.

In this mine the American Museum of Natural History excavated and removed the largest dinosaur tracks ever found.

As the road climbs upward you pass a popular ski area. Aspen groves, which twinkle like moving sunshine in the fall, line the roads. You now enter GRAND MESA NATIONAL FOREST with over 600,000 acres forested with Douglas fir, Englemann spruce, pine, aspen, oak, pinon pine and cedar.

The great MESA, with its trout-filled lakes and animal-filled forests, was the next thing to heaven to the Ute Indians, so they called this gigantic MESA "Thigusawat" (home of the departed spirits). Many lakes are easily accessible by auto. If you like to hike, ride horseback, or explore by jeep, there are innumerable remote lakes at the end of aspen and pine-shaded trails.

This great scenic wonderland is still more or less a primitive area with an altitude of 9500 to 10,500 feet above sea level and a mile above the valleys below. It's really a huge alpine meadow where flowers bloom gaily from spring until frost. Monkshood hang their blue bonnets, creamy mariposa lilies dance in the fields; red loco, purple bellflowers and golden smoke add their color. Grey sage and greasewood cover the dry flats.

GRAND MESA VILLAGE is a vacation center catering particularly to ALEXANDER, WARD, FORREST and ISLAND LAKES. The latter is stocked with yellowfin trout imported from Yellowstone National Park. LAKE VIEW POINT above ISLAND LAKE gives you a panorama of 13 of the larger lakes reflecting the blue,

Coke Ovens at the Colorado National Monument

See other photo of Monument on page 3)

blue sky.

From GRAND MESA VILLAGE our By-Way tour turns east, then north past dozens of lakes and meandering streams. This whole tableland is excellent for big game hunting with herds of elk, bear and deer available. Small game is plentiful too — sagefowl, grouse, ducks, rabbits, and pheasants.

You drop down off the MESA through COLLBRAN, then turn east through PLATEAU VALLEY.

Our By-Way tour swings southeast and again climbs the MESA. Picturesque HIGHTOWER MOUNTAIN is to the left. Again the road meanders for thirty miles through evergreen forests studded with lakes. This is real wilderness country, ideal for camping and pack trips with all the lures of that kind of vacation.

Now the road drops down off the MESA again and eventually joins State 133. Turning left, the road winds over McCLURE PASS to REDSTONE on the CRYSTAL RIVER. Beyond are CARBONDALE and ASPEN.

Our By-Way tour turns right on State 133 past PAONIA RESERVOIR and joins State 135. SOMERSET is an old coal mining community. PAONIA is situated on the North Fork of the GUNNISON RIVER.

One of the most amazing sights in the summer are the hundreds of acres of showy petunias and multi-colored snapdragons raised by the Pan-American Seed Company as part of their research project for new strains. From here the seeds are shipped to South America where they are raised for mass production.

MT. LAMBORN, seen from PAONIA, is named for the strange barren spot which resembles a lamb near the foot of the mountain.

An interesting side trip may be taken from HOTCHKISS going southeast on State 92. At CRAWFORD a side road leads past CRAWFORD RESERVOIR to the north rim of the BLACK CANYON OF THE GUNNISON (Vol. 3). State 92 continues south and east eventually ending at U. S. 50 near BLUE MESA RESERVOIR (Vol. 3).

Our By-Way tour continues on State 135 to HOTCHKISS which was named for one of the pioneers who hauled young fruit trees into the valley in spring wagons. These saplings took root and the profitable fruit industry developed. From here you follow a country road northwest around several sharp turns and climb to CEDAREDGE and once more pick up SKYWAY DRIVE to GRAND MESA VILLAGE.

From here you have two choices of roads back to GRAND JUNCTION.

One route is via LANDS END HIGHWAY which goes west past richly forested and well-stocked lakes and streams. LANDS END guards the western edge of the MESA. You'll want to stop at the Observation Building and enjoy a breathtaking view reaching for 200 miles. Before you is spread the largest canyon in the world — a mile deep and 30 miles wide which the GUNNISON and COLORADO RIVERS carved out. In the distance the mountains of Utah are hung in blue haze. The COLORADO PLATEAU sweeps majestically west and south. To the south are the LA SALS and the cloud-scratching SAN JUAN MOUNTAINS.

Now a lariat-like series of switchbacks on easy grades takes you down through ten miles of picturesque desert country. Gaudy red and yellow prickly pears and creamy yucca bells put on a spring fashion show. The road joins U. S. 50 five miles east of WHITEWATER. You continue along the GUNNISON RIVER to GRAND JUNCTION.

An alternate route from GRAND MESA VILLAGE is to remain on State 65 (SKYWAY DRIVE) going west, then north through SKYWAY which is the center for the MESA LAKES — SUNSET, MESA, JUMBO and GRIFFITH. Nearby is a popular ski area.

Now the road drops down through aspen forests which put on a sensational golden show in the autumn. The village of MESA caters to sportsmen and ranchers. Two miles beyond State 65 joins State 330.

Our By-Way tour turns west on State 65. On a ledge to the left are some interesting Ute petroglyphs. The SKYLINE DRIVE now follows winding PLATEAU CANYON with its queer rock formations. DEVILS WINGS are to the right. The camera enthusiast will find many colorful shots. The road joins U. S. 6 and 24 there, and turns southwest following the rapid flowing COLORADO RIVER to GRAND JUNCTION.

Walden and North Park

By-Way Tour No. 6

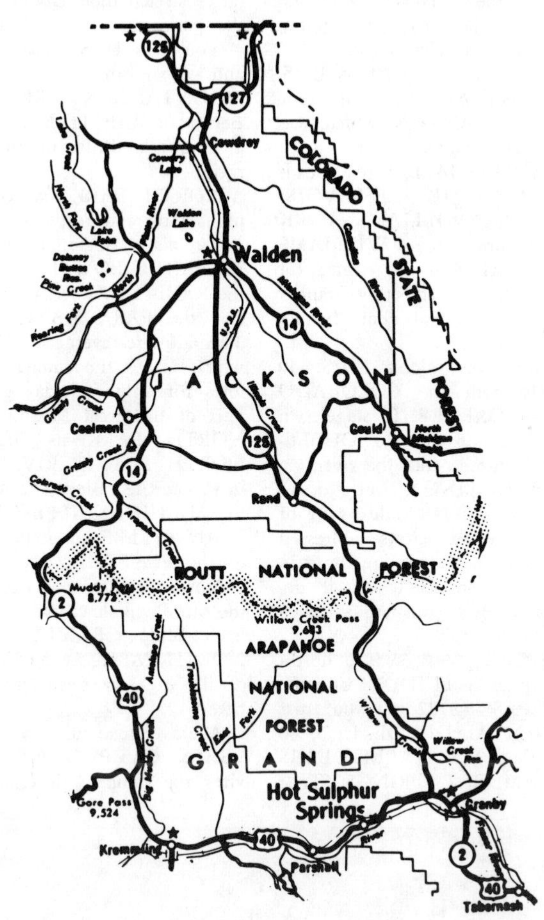

Another back country trip is followed on this By-Way tour where the average visitor can find almost any kind of mountain scenery and sport. Big game hunting and fishing are popular throughout the entire area. Much of the region is still wilderness and virgin timber country. Any trail you take off the main highway will lead you to high country spots with more than one dream of a place to camp, fish, hunt or hike. You can walk through meadows of red loco, blue monkshood and golden banner. Verdant ranches dot the rolling hills. In the autumn the aspen light up the mountainside touched by a brush dipped generously in yellow, orange and even red.

The goal of this By-Way tour is NORTH PARK, farthest north of the four mountain parks which bisect COLORADO from north to south. You start at HOT SULPHUR SPRINGS, seat of GRAND COUNTY in MIDDLE PARK. This area is noted for its incomparable mountain lettuce. The small town is a ranch and vacation center at the mouth of colorful BYERS CANYON. The Utes used the sulphur springs and wove many legends around them. Today the swimming pool, fed by the springs, is a popular spot. Skiing is a winter sport.

Our By-Way tour turns west on U. S. 40 through the red-orange sandstone cliffs of BYERS CANYON which was the old stagecoach route.

South from PARSHALL a road leads to WILLIAMS FORK RESERVOIR, then follows the WILLIAMS FORK RIVER paralleling the WILLIAMS FORK MOUNTAINS — all named for "Old" Bill Williams, an early trapper and guide. This is excellent fishing country.

You continue west along U. S. 40 which follows both the COLORADO RIVER and the D&RGRR. In stagecoach times there was a stop where TROUBLESOME CREEK empties into the river.

Next is KREMMLING (Tour No. 4) which was know as "118 miles west of Denver" and received letters addressed that way. Rudolph Kremmling built a trading post here in 1884 and it developed into today's prosperous ranch and vacation center.

From here the highway swings northwest following BIG MUDDY CREEK. At MUDDY PASS (8772 ft.) you cross the CONTINENTAL DIVIDE. U. S. 40 turns west, then tops RABBIT EARS PASS to STEAMBOAT SPRINGS (Tour No. 4).

On the crest of MUDDY PASS you can gaze down into NORTH PARK which looks like a beautiful green bowl. Beneath you the world stretches to the north in undulating, endless fashion. The NORTH PLATTE RIVER and its tributaries stretch their crooked fingers across the park.

You leave U. S. 40 at MUDDY PASS and go north on State 14. BAKER MOUNTAIN SKI AREA is to the left. Beyond is RABBIT EARS MOUNTAIN, a unique upthrust of two slim granite rocks.

NORTH PARK, which is forty-five miles long and forty-two miles wide, is in a giant horseshoe formed by the MEDICINE BOW RANGE to the east, the RABBIT EARS RANGE to the south, and the PARK RANGE to the west. The altitude averages about 7800 feet which makes the summer short and allows for only a 60-day growing period. Part of the great Missouri River Basin, NORTH PARK is drained by the NORTH PLATTE RIVER which heads in this fertile valley. The torturous, winding MICHIGAN, ILLINOIS and CANADIAN RIVERS are important tributaries to the PLATTE.

Now the highway drops down into the cattle and sheep ranch country following BIG GRIZZLY CREEK into NORTH PARK. An oil field to the right of the highway seems most incongruous here.

A gravel road turns west to GRIZZLY CREEK CAMP GROUNDS which invites the camper, fisherman and hunter

Colorado's majestic mountains dramatically punctuate forest-framed meadows below

to stop anywhere and make himself at home. Another road leads south from this route to COALMONT. The discovery of a form of lignite coal close to the surface brought more miners into the PARK last century.

You stay on State 14 to WALDEN, only town of any size in NORTH PARK. Seat of JACKSON COUNTY, it is a ranching and vacation headquarters. A frontier-type western town set on a gravelly plain, WALDEN comes to life mainly in the summer when thousands of trout fishermen come in for the superb sport. It's actually at a wilderness crossroads which divides NORTH PARK in half but quadruples the scenery.

Northeast of town on a dirt road in the McCallum Oil Field is the unique "Ice Cream Well." Oil drillers struck a mixture of oil and carbon dioxide which registers a constant 136 degrees below zero. As a result, the pipe lines and machinery are always coated with a yellow frost which resembles vanilla ice cream.

Several side trips may be taken from WALDEN. One follows State 125 straight north along the MICHIGAN RIVER where sleek, fat cattle graze knee-deep in luxuriant hay meadows. Huge red sandstone "sand dunes" border the MEDICINE BOW RANGE to the right. COWDREY is another vacation and ranch supply center.

Another side trip goes north from COWDREY. Just outside of town where the highway crosses the railroad tracks you can see the Ozark-Mahoning Fluorspar Mill operating at NORTHGATE. A few miles north of here the highway divides. State 125 swings west and north across the Colorado-Wyoming border to Encampment, Wyoming.

The other road, State 127, turns right. PINKHAM is named for a pioneer, James O. Pinkham, first white settler, who built an old log cabin here in 1876. He panned gold in the streams nearby and his tales brought other miners. North along a narrow, winding dirt road is the Two Hundred Level Mine where fluorspar is dug and shipped to NORTHGATE for milling. Fluorspar has become a strategic mineral since missiles are being built. The ore is made into fluorine, a violently active chemical, used in uranium separation and to make rocket fuels. COLORADO is second to southern Illinois in fluorspar production. Interesting specimen may be found here by the rockhound.

The highway continues east through varicolored KINGS CANYON, then turns north. If you are really interested in off-the-beaten-path country, choose any one of the several dirt roads which take off from State 127. They meander across picturesque high plateau country populated only by wandering herds of sheep on summer pasture. One route going east from MOUNTAIN HOME (Wyo. State 230) will take you through the famous CHIMNEY ROCK country, a fantastic array of red-colored rocks, which was a hideout for road agents and cattle thieves in the early days.

Another side trip goes southeast on State 14 from WALDEN following the MICHIGAN RIVER. As the road approaches the summit of CAMERON PASS, you climb easy grades through dense stands of lodgepole pine. Be sure to notice where the forests have been thinned to allow new growth.

Our By-Way tour takes State 125 south from WALDEN where it picks up the twisting ILLINOIS RIVER and follows it to its source. This is excellent fishing and hunting country. RAND, named for a frontier scout, caters to visitors.

A narrow dirt road goes east from RAND to the ghost town of TELLER CITY, built in 1879, where silver deposits were discovered. The ENDOMILE MINE was the biggest producer. TELLER CITY was a large town as may be seen by the many houses and sagging foundations, all gradually disintegrating. Foot and horse trails skirt MT. RICHTOFEN over LULU PASS to GASKILL, DUTCHTOWN and LULU which flourished at the same time as TELLER CITY.

You continue south from RAND on State 125 across sage-strewn rolling hills and top the RABBIT EARS MOUNTAINS at WILLOW CREEK PASS (9683 alt.).

Now State 125 drops down into the COLORADO RIVER VALLEY where it joins U. S. 40. You may turn east three miles to GRANBY (Tour No. 2).

A right turn on U. S. 40 takes you through lovely pine-scented forests back to HOT SULPHUR SPRINGS.

Dinosaur National Monument and Trappers Lake

By-Way Tour No. 7

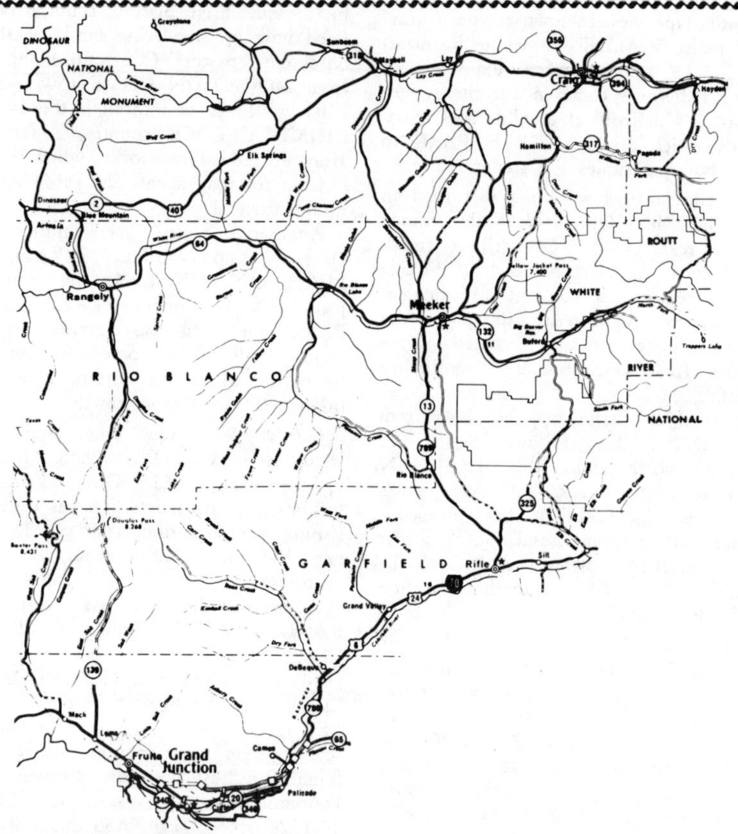

The northwestern section of COLORADO is an interesting combination of rolling, sage-dotted hills and colored canyons, irrigated fields and vast ranches, high peaks and flat mesas, immense coal fields and a gigantic dinosaur graveyard.

Our By-Way tour starts in CRAIG (U. S. 40), seat of MOFFAT COUNTY, and built in the late 1880's in the wide valley of the YAMPA RIVER. Crossroads of a great ranching, oil and scenic empire, CRAIG remained a "cow town" until the development of coal beds, oil and gas fields, gilsonite mines and copper deposits with uranium being its latest mineral.

Agriculture is still the basic industry, however. Large irrigated and dryland ranches produce prodigious crops of wheat, alfalfa, potatoes, and vegetables. Great cattle and sheep ranches add to its prosperity with the town being one of the largest sheep rail shipping points in the U.S.

Be sure to see David Moffat's private railroad car, now the Chamber of Commerce's Hospitality Center, in the City Park. This western railroad giant dreamed of a tunnel under the CONTINENTAL DIVIDE and a railroad to the Pacific.

The MOFFAT TUNNEL (Tour No. 2) was realized, but the railroad ended at CRAIG.

To the east of town is HAYDEN (U. S. 40), built in 1874, another shipping point for sheep where homesteaders came in the early 1900's and built a prosperous community.

Our By-Way tour turns south from CRAIG following the YAMPA RIVER for several miles until the latter makes a sharp right turn northwest to its rendezvous with the GREEN RIVER. HAMILTON is the site of some of the early oil fields in the district.

State 317, a scenic road, turns east through back country, following the WILLIAMS FORK RIVER through PAGODA, WILLOW CREEK and PINNACLE to OAK CREEK (Tour No. 4).

Four miles south of HAMILTON another side road continues straight south past THORNBURG MOUNTAIN (right) and the granite THORNBURG MEMORIAL, site of the battle between the U. S. Cavalry under Major T. T. Thornburg and the rebellious Utes who were hidden on the bluffs above RED CANYON. The troops were enroute to MEEKER where there had been an Indian uprising. The major and several soldiers were killed, but the troops finally barricaded themselves with the supply train and withstood a three-day seige before they were rescued. West of the highway are some Indian pictographs on the canyon walls. Arrowheads are found here. The road joins State 13 near MEEKER.

You continue south on State 13 past ILES GROVE on the creek bottom. AXIAL and STREETER are set in the midst of vast undeveloped coal fields although there are some working mines.

The town of MEEKER is midway between RIFLE and CRAIG. The town always celebrates the 4th of July with the RANGE CALL RODEO, reminiscent of old-time celebrations complete with bands, fireworks, pink lemonade and horse-racing. Today MEEKER is a successful ranching and vacation center with the added impetus of the proximity of COLORADO'S largest oil and gas fields opening to the west. The potential wealth of this region is stupendous.

Historic MEEKER on the banks of the WHITE RIVER was named for the man who precipitated the infamous MEEKER MASSACRE in 1879. Nathan C. Meeker, Indian agent and friend of Horace Greeley, was unfitted to handle the Utes who grew more and more hostile as the Federal Government failed to live up to its treaties with them. When Meeker, who tried to make farmers out of the wandering tribes, finally plowed an irrigation ditch across the track where they raced their ponies, the revolt started under Chiefs Colorow, Douglas and Captain Jackson. Meeker and ten men were massacred while his wife and daughter and another woman and her children were seized as hostages. Chief Ouray of the southern Utes finally helped rescue them a month later.

MEEKER is the gateway to the upper WHITE RIVER country with over a hundred fishable lakes abounding in gamey trout and whitefish. Take State 132 east following the WHITE RIVER to BUFORD, vacation center.

From TWIN SPRINGS RANCH the highway is graveled and curves up to a fork. The left hand road follows RIPPLE CREEK, a favorite motor trip during the autumn when this high country flames with fall's golden aspen. Breathtaking views of the WHITE RIVER VALLEY are spread below. The road leads to WILLOW CREEK and OAK CREEK.

You continue along the road to TRAPPERS LAKE, considered one of the most pictorial spots in COLORADO. Here are miles of undulating pine-clad shore-line providing the plug fisherman or fly caster with quiet coves. This is the place where the fisherman's tall tales become facts. Some of the conifer forests, unfortunately, were killed by a beetle infestation a few years ago; but the country is still rugged and spectacular. A five mile trail winds east to LITTLE TRAPPERS LAKE, then north to DEVILS CAUSEWAY, a high narrow basalt ridge.

Another side trip from MEEKER follows State 64 west along the WHITE RIVER past the MEEKER MONUMENT, a pink granite slab about three miles west of town, the approximate site of the massacre. Seven miles west of town a dirt road turns south through SCENERY GULCH DETOUR, a fantastically eroded canyon of weird idols, castles, and temple-shaped formations. The road rejoins State 64 near WHITE RIVER CITY, site of one of the first white settlements, with only a tiny schoolhouse to mark the spot. Straight south from here following PICEANCE (long grass) CREEK are 26,000 acres maintained by the COLORADO GAME AND FISH DEPARTMENT where they study the largest deer herd in North America. During hunting season the area is open without restrictions from landowners. This road is a popular one in the spring when visitors from all over come to watch thousands of deer grazing en route to their summer range in the mountains.

From WHITE RIVER CITY the highway curves up past another Ute battlefield where the Indians made one last attempt in 1887 to retake their COLORADO hunting ground. Led by Chief Colorow, they were defeated and driven back to their reservation in Utah. Next is RANGELY.

Our By-Way tour follows State 13 south from MEEKER to RIO BLANCO

Dinosaur National Monument is a land of fantasy encompassing amazing rock formations, weird canyons and gnarled ghost-like trees

where it crosses PICEANCE CREEK. Gas and oil fields dot the valley. Colorful ROAN PLATEAU to the west is a vast oil shale reserve containing an estimated 300 million barrels of oil. RIFLE SKI CENTER is to the right.

You join I 70 at RIFLE and turn southwest following the swiftly moving COLORADO RIVER (excellent fishing).

The scenic road north from DE BEQUE along ROAN CREEK to ROAN CLIFFS leads to good fishing and hunting country and shows off the various strata of the country spectacularly. The BOOK CLIFFS are a Paleocene boneyard yielding some of the world's best specimen of insect and fish fossils. Every strata of the earth's crust is exposed — a real geological layer cake which becomes a giant textbook. This is another entrance to the nation's richest, largest and most accessible oil shale fields. Left from DE BEQUE is the PAINT POT COUNTRY or the DEVILS PLAYGROUND which also contains fossils and Indian artifacts.

Leaving DE BEQUE on Interstate 70 follow DE BEQUE CANYON. The canyon walls were once picturesquely studded with cliff swallows' mud nests. Unfortunately when the new highway was built, many of the nests were destroyed. Watch for them on undisturbed canyon walls.

At MESA JUNCTION State 65 turns left to GRAND MESA (Tour No. 5). GRAND VALLEY is a fruit center. PALISADE is the hub of the peach industry in the GRAND VALLEY. Warm winds funnel up the valley between the high cliffs to encourage a long growing season.

GRAND JUNCTION, largest city in western COLORADO, is known for both fruit and uranium (Tour No. 5).

Our By-Way tour continues northwest on U. S. 6 and 24 to FRUITA in the broad lower GRAND VALLEY, also a fruit and vegetable center. COLORADO NATIONAL MONUMENT (Tour No. 5) is south on State 340.

Six miles west of FRUITA is LOMA where you turn north on State 139. The highway climbs up SALT CREEK CANYON cutting through the BOOK CLIFFS, then angles through BROWN'S CANYON and swings to the top of DOUGLAS CREEK PASS (8000 feet) where you get an imposing view of the entire area.

To the west of DOUGLAS PASS in the serrated cliffs, hills and shadowed ravines are the greatest gilsonite deposits in the world. This freak of nature, solid carbon, was first used to make special varnishes, marine cable wrappings, floor tile, storage battery cases, and inks. Now, in addition, it is changed to electrolytic or calcined coke, high octane gasoline and fuel oil. When first discovered in 1884 in great perpendicular veins, it was worked by hand, but today everything is mechanized.

State 139 drops down from the pass along wide switchbacks with a stunning view of the green ribbon of WHITE RIVER VALLEY in the distance. RANGELY is a late boom town. Founded in 1880 as a trading post, the town mushroomed after World War II when the large gas and oil fields and the gilsonite mines began to be developed. Now RANGELY is COLORADO'S largest oil producing area, but still a raw frontier town.

Our By-Way tour swings northwest from RANGELY on State 64 to ARTESIA and picks up U.S. 40. You turn west and cross the Colorado-Utah State Line 12 miles to Jensen, Utah. Then turn north about seven miles to unique DINOSAUR NATIONAL MONUMENT, a land of unspoiled, primitive beauty.

The QUARRY VISITOR CENTER is here with its unusual dinosaur quarry showing graphically the world in which the "terrible lizards" lived. Rock layers have been removed to illustrate the fossil-bearing Morrison formation of the Jurassic era which was deposited some 140 million years ago. A three-mile dirt road leads to SPLIT MOUNTAIN GORGE.

Our By-Way tour continues east on U. S. 40 through ARTESIA, MASSADONE and curves northeast to ELK SPRINGS. Another dirt road takes off here northwest to YAMPA BENCH where another trail leads to HELL'S CANYON, BEAR'S CANYON and CASTLE PARK.

From CROSS MOUNTAIN U. S. 40 continues to MAYBELL, where the adventurous leave the main highway to the launching area of thrilling boat trips through the inaccessible flaming canyons of the YAMPA and GREEN RIVERS.

Take State 318 northwest through SUNBEAM to the rugged grandeur of the DEEP CANYON COUNTRY, rich in cattle rustling lore and offering thrills of exploration to the modern adventurer. The semi-arid rolling desert country has only sage, rabbit brush and mesquite for cover, with deep arroyos scarring the earth.

Continue on State 318 to another fork where the highway turns north going through scenic IRISH CANYON. To the left is DIAMOND PEAK at the north end of BROWN'S PARK where in 1872 one of the most colossal frauds was ever perpetuated. Two men "salted' or planted some diamonds, emeralds, rubies and other precious gems on the high, rocky plateau. Then they sold stock and fleeced hundreds of thousands of dollars out of gullible people before the hoax was discovered.

At the junction you take the dirt road west for about nine miles, then turn left sharply and wind down across COTTONWOOD CREEK to BROWN'S PARK, originally known as BROWN'S HOLE, named for a French-Canadian trapper of the 1830's. It was a fur trappers' rendezvous for many years, later becoming the hideout of the notorious Butch Cassidy and his gang of cattle rustlers and train robbers.

Here begins the spectacular LODORE CANYON of the GREEN RIVER, named by General William Ashley in 1825. Its dark red, cedar-studded, perpendicular cliffs shoot 2,000 feet above the foaming, churning river. Prepare to be stunned by the visual and photographic treat ahead. Between May 1 and August 1, one to six-day boat trips may be made (write ahead for reservations). Horseback trips are available.

The water trip goes through deep and awe-inspiring narrow canyons formed by the GREEN and YAMPA RIVERS. A paradise of color and exotic land forms, this new wonderland of scenic beauty is rivaled only by the GRAND CANYON. Most of the terrain is so rugged and primitive that it is accessible only by foot, horseback, jeep or boats.

Return from BROWN'S PARK through GREYSTONE to SUNBEAM and MAYBELL. U. S. 40 goes east through LAY and returns to CRAIG.

ABOUT THE AUTHORS

It was natural for Iris Gilmore and Marian Talmadge to write COLORADO HI-WAYS AND BY-WAYS. They have either driven, hiked, gone by jeep or horseback, or flown over practically every square mile of COLORADO. They are particularly interested in the "By-Ways" with the result that they have explored almost every nook and cranny in the state. In addition, they have collected dozens of stories from "old-timers" to use in books and articles.

Mrs. Gilmore and Mrs. Talmadge have also collaborated on other writing projects. In addition to articles and short stories, they have written several books. Among them are four books about the United States Air Force Academy — the most popular being THIS IS THE AIR FORCE ACADEMY, published by Dodd, Mead. Their book, PONY EXPRESS BOY, won the $2000 BOY'S LIFE — DODD, MEAD prize competition for the United States and Canada. They have also written the first book about NORAD, THE NORTH AMERICAN AIR DEFENSE COMMAND, which tells the story of the fabulous underground detection system for the protection of the United States and Canada located deep in the heart of Cheyenne Mountain near Colorado Springs, Colorado.

ACKNOWLEDGMENTS

Denver & Rio Grande Western Railroad
Denver Convention & Visitors' Bureau
Denver Public Library, Western Collection
State of Colorado Advertising & Publicity Dept.
Colorado State Historical Society